To: M.L. Willis
and the greatest gifts I have ever manifested, Charli and Parker Mason.

TABLE OF CONTENTS

INTRODUCTION
Delish-ism

When you live life on your own terms, you have few regrets.

Not my mother's life
Doing it my way
Fed a dream, not a path
Getting to deliciousness

CHAPTER 2
Delish-ism

If you have been doing something for 365 days and on day 366 you realize it is not working, don't waste time worrying about the 365 days, focus on day 367.

Rock bottom, autopilot and other foolishness that keeps you from having what you want
Limited Thinking: The *Hater* within
What's really holding you back?

CHAPTER 3
Delish-ism

Me First. You Second. In that Order.

Loving yourself to the core
Give to You
No is the new yes in a delicious life
Real control is letting go of the need for control

CHAPTER 4
Delish-ism

I am about 50 percent perfect, but 100 percent real.

Flaws and all
Recognize the gap between the real and the ideal
Looks are everything

Delish-ism

Having a bottomless bank account is not enough to create true prosperity—although it helps. You must believe you deserve all of the money and resources that are flowing into your life.

What's your money story?
Give the poverty mentality the boot
Go to (financial) rehab
Ready, set financial goals
A cheat sheet to financial prosperity

Delish-ism
You have to feel good to do better.

Happiness for smart women
Get your mind right
Weight watching and hip consequences
That's for white people and other fatty lies

Delish-ism
Whenever you're ready, love will seek you out.

Are you ready for love?
The real you in relationships
Letting go of what you never received

Delish-ism
Be about it. The Way will open up.

Delish-ism

When you live life on your own terms,

you have few regrets.

I have always been an out-of-the-box kind of girl. From my asymmetrical haircut in the 1990s to my rhinestone stilettos today, I have always known what works for me. If I wanted to do something, I did it. If I didn't want to do something, I didn't do it. It was as simple as that—or, I should say, as *selfish* as that.

Now, I know what you are thinking: *being selfish is wrong and self-centered. What about the people in my life who need me—my children, my partner, my boss, my family, my friends?* Yes, they need you, but you need you more.

There have been countless books written about how to get to the top or become successful, often focused on strategies such as networking or setting clear goals. However, very few books let you in on the real secret to success and happiness—making you the number one priority in your own life. *Me First* does just that.

Me First is an approach to living—a deliciously selfish approach to getting what you want in life without excuses, regrets, or apologies. Before making any decision—getting into a relationship or choosing a career path—you will start with the most important question: What do I want? The second question you will ask is: How does this decision, action, or choice benefit me directly? If it's not what you want or does not benefit you directly, don't do it. *How selfish,* you say. I agree.

In the best-case scenario (which almost never happens, BTW), what you want and what benefits you the most is in alignment with what others want from you. The problem arises when there is a conflict between what you want or desire and what others want from you. Rather than being guided by your own hopes and dreams, you become hemmed in by the hopes and desires that others have projected onto you.

When most women are faced with the tough choice of them or me, we usually choose them. They—our children, partner, family, boss, or friends—need us more than we need ourselves. As a result, our wants, needs and desires become secondary. The reasons we choose them over us are many. It may be fear, guilt, lack of self-worth, feeling undeserving of having our needs met, or at a very basic level, disbelieve that we have the right to be happy or fulfilled in our own lives.

At the heart of *Me First* is the belief that you have the right to be happy, fulfilled, and live life on your own terms, whatever those terms may be. If you want to be a stay-at-home mom, great. If you want to start your own business or to become an actor, do it. If you love being single and don't want children or a husband, own it. It's your life. Live deliciously and you'll get whatever it is you want.

Not My Mother's Life

My mother is an extraordinary woman. I marvel at how she was able to raise four children on a shoestring budget with very little thanks. Her life has revolved around three things: her man, her children, and her job. She has never been on a real vacation, to a spa or to a fancy restaurant more than a handful of times. In spite of these realities, she has rarely complained. On autopilot, she has always done what it takes to get things done.

I think it is safe to say that my mother did not live a deliciously selfish life. I am sure she experienced moments of joy and happiness. I am just certain that it was not *delicious*. I believe women of her generation who lived deliciously selfish lives were the exception and not the rule. Think Chaka Khan, Tina Turner (post-Ike), Shirley Chisholm, and Oprah Winfrey. These women were trailblazers in their own right and not just because they achieved fame or fortune. They pushed against all the barriers that surrounded them and went after what they wanted. Even more, they also weren't afraid to fail or to make mistakes along the way. It took guts and a whole lot more for Anna Mae Bullock, *aka* Tina Turner, to leave Nutbush, Tennessee, where she was born and raised, to pursue a singing career. And it takes even more ovaries to run for the President of the United States as Shirley Chisholm did in 1972. They just went for it.

Doing It My Way

For the most part, the expectations for my life were carved out before I could have ever begun to imagine what I could want for myself. As a brown-skinned girl born to a teenage mother, growing up in and around Los Angeles in the late 1970s, the bar for my success was set very low. No one in my family had finished high school, and because we were poor, I did not expect much more than what I had, which, to be honest, was very little.

As a teenager, I remember catching the bus to high-end shopping malls to try on clothes. Looking in the mirror, I'd say to myself, *"one day I'm going to be able to come in here and buy whatever I want."* I also recall practicing my signature for when I'd become a lawyer and would need to sign important documents. Although, I didn't become a lawyer and instead obtained my PhD, it's still my signature today.

At the age of seventeen, I left home with one bag of clothes and the shoes on my feet to work at the Riviera Hotel and Casino in Las Vegas, Nevada. It was on that dusty bus ride between California and the Nevada desert that I made the decision to live life on my own terms. As far as I could tell, there were only two choices: cave in to expectations or create my own way. Caving in was not an option.

While in Las Vegas, I continued to work during the evenings and attended school during the day. And my determination paid off. In 1994, I applied to Howard University in Washington, DC and was awarded a full merit scholarship. Before that point in my life, I had never been on a plane or out of the protective cocoon of my community. It was incredible, and I never looked back.

To be sure, I did not see anyone around me living the life I wanted or desired to live. I had no context for anything more than I already had in my life. However, through my experiences and, even more, the loving and admirable women who came into my life, I learned that you can create your life just the way you want, even if you don't have a road map or if no one has ever done it before.

Fed a Dream, Not a Path

Like many girls of my generation, I was fed the slightly revised fairytale of marriage, the suburban Colonial home, 2.5 children, and a high-powered career—*Claire Huxtable made it look so easy.* However, I think many of us have come to realize that while this fairytale might exist, it is not for everyone. *Me*

First asks you to break the mold and to write your own script of happiness, love, and success. What does your "happily ever after" look like?

Getting to Deliciousness

As Black women, we live in a society that fails to validate our beauty, needs, hopes, and dreams. I can count on one hand the positive reflections of African-American women in the media and in our culture. We have also gotten mixed messages about how to be, act, and feel. You are either too independent or you are a gold digger. You are a vixen or a good girl. You are *wifey* material or a *jump off*. You are either too full of yourself or allow people to treat you like a doormat. It can be crazy making.

I have talked to many of my girlfriends all of whom, at some point or another, have felt burnt out, unloved, undesired, unappreciated, unfocused, or unfulfilled. When asked why, many of them really do not have an answer, or the answer is outside of them. It is their partner, their children, their career, their boss, their finances . . . the list can go on and on. Many of them are moving so quickly and really have not set aside the space and time to ask: *What is it that I really want? I understand that I am moving, but am I moving in the direction I want to go, with whom I want to go, or for the purposes I want moving me?*

Getting to a deliciously selfish life requires you to take a step back from the craziness to figure out who you are and what you want. Maybe you will discover that although you have been playing the role of the good girl, you are really a vixen. Perhaps you will figure out that although you are independent and can take care of yourself, you enjoy being pampered with gifts and treats from your partner. The idea is to figure it out for yourself and once you do, to own it.

Living deliciously is also about being fearless, taking risks, and choosing your own path. The goal is to not to have a perfect life or to be perfect as defined by society or by others, but to have a life that you can be proud of and one that is a true reflection of your passions, your commitments, and the core of who you are.

The deliciously selfish woman is confident, insecure, ambitious, spontaneous, meticulous, awkward, and real—all at the same time. She is okay with the contradictions and the parts of herself that are a little jagged or sharp. She is able to laugh, admit when something's not working, try harder the next time around, and above all, to keep it moving.

Living deliciously is not for the faint of heart. It demands discipline. In most cases, you will have to put the people in your life on notice. There is a new you in town and she is serious about living selfishly. In the process, you might discover things about yourself that are not so delicious, things that get to the core of what's been holding you back from having what you want. That's fine too.

Creating and living a deliciously selfish life is a journey. You must be willing to put in the work to get the life that you want. There are no shortcuts. *Me First* shows you how to get from where you are to where you want to be by using Delish-isms focused on the areas of your life that matter most: relationships, careers, health, and finances. There are also kick starters and things to try at the end of each chapter. But enough build up, let's get started.

CHAPTER 2

Delish~ism

If you have been doing something for 365 days

and on day 366 you realize it is not working,

don't waste time worrying about the 365 days,

focus on day 367.

It is easy to realize that you need to make a change when you have hit rock bottom, or when you look up and see you have alienated your friends and family because of bad behavior; or because you've lost your job, partner, home, or something else of value to you. These are the times when you say, *Okay, something is not working here and I have to figure this out quickly.* The losses are so great or painful that there is no denying the need for a change or a major shift.

It is harder, though, to figure out that you need to make a change when you are on autopilot or just going through the motions of life. When you are on autopilot, there are a lot of distractions or external things that occupy your time and life. These distractions can come in the guise of material possessions, your career, your partner, food, sex, or an entire host of other things. It is the going, going and going and when you stop the silence is so heavy or deafening that you start moving again to keep from having to deal with what started you moving in the first place. It is that deep soul feeling that something's just not right, but I cannot quite put my finger on it or rather I refuse to put my finger on it.

Whatever you have going on right now or whatever changes you want to make in your life, you just have to get started. Make the decision to have what you want in your life. If you want to end a relationship or find a partner; quit a job or find a career; lose weight or get your finances in order—just do it!

Are you having a panic attack yet? Are you thinking about all of the reasons why what you want is impossible? *It's hard. I'll look like a fool. I don't have the time. What will people say? My life is fine the way it is, really.* I can hear you now. This is good. That is the fear, resistance, and guilt coming up. You will have to deal with this fear and resistance if you are going to have a deliciously selfish life. Let's talk about it.

Resistance

Resistance is tricky because it never looks the way we expect it to look. In our lives, it shows up as busyness or not enough time. When we do not want to do something, we can always find a hundred different reasons to put it off and they all seem legitimate. I am guilty of this myself. If I do not want to do something,

I create a crisis that must be dealt with immediately. I call my friends, family, and even old co-workers to see what is going on in their lives: *certainly they need my help or a listening ear.* Other resistance tactics include deep cleaning your house, car, or desk; taking on extra responsibilities at work, church, or in your community; or making a mental checklist about why things are fine just the way they are.

Resistance to getting what you want is based on your personal history. It is shaped by your beliefs about how changes or shifts will impact your life emotionally, materially, and physically. It may also be based on how others in your life might perceive or react to the changes or your desire to prioritize your needs in your own life. *The nerve of you.*

For example, if you want to end a relationship that is no longer working for you, but your friends or family members don't think it is a good idea, you might hesitate to rock the boat. It is normal to have anxiety about getting started, how others might react to your new life or direction, or what is on the other side of the decision. The key to overcoming the resistance is to recognize it, own it, and to push through it.

Once you begin to live a deliciously selfish life, the most important opinion will be yours and the ultimate decision maker will be YOU.

Guilt

Our lives are the sum of our choices. Some choices are small, such as deciding what to have for lunch, and others have the power to change the trajectory of our lives, such as going to college, getting married, moving across the country, having a child, or quitting a job.

In times when you believe you have made the wrong choice, behaved badly or wronged someone you care deeply for, guilt can set in. We also feel guilty if we believe that we have let others down or if we fail to meet the expectations of our family, friends, colleagues, or partners. Women, more than men, are likely to feel guilty if we are unable to be all things to all people at all times. We allow the expectations, needs, and desires of other people to shape our choices and behaviors, and when we can't live up to or meet them, we beat ourselves up. As a feeling, guilt is very powerful and can be all-consuming.

Guilt can also be accompanied by feelings of shame, embarrassment, or even unworthiness. Like guilt, these emotions are useless and prevent you from seeing what is possible in your life today. Guilt and the feelings associated with it, however, are only as powerful as you allow them to be in your life. You can honor your past as just that, the past, rather than seeing it as the sole indicator of what you are capable of achieving in your life right now.

To move past the guilt, you have to release or find closure around the times in your life when you acted out of fear, anger, anxiety, or any other negative space. You know the times: *Like that time when you got so drunk you accused your best friend of trying to steal your man. Or that time when you were called out by your sister at Thanksgiving and you cussed out everybody at the dinner table.* Yes, those times.

The truth is, you can only know what you know at any given time. Your past is only a brief reflection of where you were during a particular moment in time, working with a set of tools and resources you had available to you then, but not now. Today, you are working to create a new awareness, to sharpen your emotional skill set, and to start over.

There is no room for guilt in the deliciously selfish life. Truly living life on your own terms requires releasing the guilt associated with past choices, behaviors, or experiences. I am not suggesting you should not apologize for mistreating someone or for being *"foul"*; it is just to say that once you have atoned for the behavior, let it go.

Belief That It's Too Late to Make a Change

It is never too late to make a change or to start living the life that you want. As we get older, we begin to realize that every decision, good or bad, we have made along the way has gotten us to where we are today. As a result, we begin to believe that change is impossible, and even if it is possible, it won't make a difference. Many of us understand time as an investment or as something that has meaning for its own sake. As crazy as it sounds, many of us would rather keep doing something that does not work because of the time already invested than to admit it's not working or that we are unfulfilled by it.

> **I had a baby at the age of 16 and by 18 I had another. Now, I'm 26 with two kids, without a high school diploma, and in a dead-end job. I don't know even know where to begin.**
>
> For the past 10 years, you've probably had to prioritize providing for your children and making ends meet. Now that your children are a bit older and in school full-time, slowly begin to focus on your needs and goals. Sign up for a class to obtain your high school diploma during the evenings or on the weekend. Once you get your GED, look into further training or into enrolling at a local community college.
>
> To get back on track you have to start somewhere. You will also have to make adjustments to your daily routine—getting up early or staying up late—in order to make the shifts and changes in your life that will get you to your next level. You will also need a solid support system filled with family, friends, and other moms who are also working toward similar goals.

Your choices should never feel like a life sentence. You have the right to change your mind and to chart a new path if your current one is not leading you to where you want to go. If a situation is not in your best interest, no matter if it's a job, a marriage, or a relationship, it is your right to choose again.

Stuck in the Familiar

When something is familiar, it can feel comfortable and right. Chaos and drama, for example, can feel normal if that is all you have ever known or experienced in your life. If you grew up in a home that was hurtful, unloving, or unsupportive, it is not unrealistic to imagine that you will create relationships and situations that affirm your feelings about families or relationships. If you find yourself in a situation that is different from what you are used to, it will feel uncomfortable or unfamiliar.

The familiar can also shape your expectations of yourself and others. If you have been mistreated in the past or have had low expectations for what is possible in your life, the bar for how others should treat you will also be very low. You will accept less than what you deserve because in the past you have not gotten what you want. If you have had partners that have treated you as if you were disposable, or if you have earned less than what you were worth, then it is not unreasonable that you might expect the same in the future.

> **I have worked at the same company for the past six years without a raise. When I asked my boss for a small increase, she told me that I barely earned my current salary and that I should be lucky to have a job. I just feel so stuck.**
>
> ---
>
> Ouch. Stepping up to ask for what you want, even when your knees shake and your voice quivers, is always a good thing. We have no control over how others respond to our requests or if they will say yes to what it is that we want.
>
> Your boss actually did you a favor. Her response should serve as a wake-up call and provide you with all the information you need to figure out what is that you require in your next job or work situation to be happy and fulfilled. While you might have anxiety about how difficult it will be to find another job, staying in a situation that doesn't feel good or that chips away at your self-worth will only make matters worse.

In living a deliciously selfish life, you must be willing to move beyond your current circumstances to create the life that you want. If you want a better relationship or a better job, you have to raise the bar and step out your comfort zone. You will have to change the way you see and value yourself, as well as what you can expect from others in your life. This is a huge step.

In creating your new life, there will be parts of you that no longer serve you well and you will have to release those parts so that you can have what you want. In the process of releasing, give yourself permission to mourn the loss of your old self and to appreciate how your former self got you through difficult times.

Limited Thinking: The Hater Within

As the saying goes, *Haters gon' hate.* The question is what happens when the thing that is holding you back is not other people, but your own limited thinking about having what you can have in your life?

Limited or negative thinking is the belief that you will never aspire to more than what you already have, or focusing on the reasons why you cannot have what you want, instead of emphasizing the reasons why you can. Limited thinking is like walking around with blinders on that only allow you to see what is missing and where you came from. With these blinders on, it is difficult to see all of the possibilities surrounding you, because your focus is on that which you lack and the past.

The reason limited thinking is so dangerous is that it is often hardwired into our brains or our subconscious from a very early age. We receive messages of deficiencies and limitations from society, our community, the media, and in some instances, from those who are critical to our emotional development like our parents, which is why in our adult life these messages are still present and influencing our behavior and actions.

If you have ever believed you were ugly, unattractive, fat, not good enough, stupid, too dark, too light, or nappy headed, the chances are that you received negative messages early on in life and internalized them. If you did not have anyone around you to counter the negative messages, more than likely they have influenced your perception of people, the world, and what is possible in your life. With a limited perspective of what is possible, you can talk yourself out of anything before it ever has a chance to happen.

Everyone I've ever dated has cheated on me or been verbally abusive. Now, I expect to be cheated on and begin to look for clues early on in the relationship to confirm my suspicions. How can I change this?

You can begin by taking a step back and reflecting on your early experiences of intimate relationships and partnerships. Were they respectful and loving or hurtful and abusive? This matters. Our dating relationships and partnership are a reflection of how we feel about ourselves, our deepest wounds and insecurities, and our early relationships including those with our parents.

To bring a different relationship experience into your life, you have to be willing to be honest about what's driving your insecurities and attraction to individuals who don't treat you well. Once you do, you will able begin to make choices from a healthier and more self-affirming place.

A huge part of living a deliciously selfish life is doing away with limited thinking and those negative messages that have kept us from receiving love, success, and happiness in our lives. If you don't believe your own hype, nobody else will.

What's Really Holding You Back?

To live deliciously, you have to be honest about what's holding you back from having what you want. Is it your boss? Is it your partner? Is it your children? Is it your past? It is your lack of training or education? Is it your bank account? Is it past mistakes? Is it your looks?

If you answered 'yes' to any of the above questions, you'd be wrong. The only thing, person or issue holding you back from having what you want is you. What keeps us from having what we want or from getting started are the stories we tell ourselves about who we are and what we can be and have in our lives. It's also about how we allow those stories to shape, control, and influence our actions and what we believe is possible.

The stories we tell ourselves about what we can have are based on our past experiences, our childhood, and our current lives or circumstances. For example, if you were cheated on in a relationship, your story might be that all of the good ones are taken or that you're unworthy of love. If you grew up in poverty, your story might be that money is hard to come by and that you will always have to struggle to make ends meet. In both scenarios, what you want—a good relationship and money in the bank—are shaped by what you've experienced in the past.

The stories we weave about our past experiences and the reasons why we can't have what we want are nothing more than excuses to keep us from getting started or getting back into the game. There are countless examples of individuals who have grown up in poverty and are now millionaires or otherwise successful. We've also known people who have had one bad relationship after another and are now in happy and fulfilling relationships. What you want is possible even if your past has shown you otherwise.

In Summary

The first step to living a deliciously selfish is life is to be willing to jump right in and get started. Your life up to this point has been filled with choices, lessons and experiences that have gotten you to this moment. Resistance, guilt, fear and limited thinking will come up, but your job is to move through it all so that you can have what you want in your life.

KICK STARTERS AND THINGS TO TRY

Take Inventory. What does your current life look like in the four major areas: relationships, finances, health, and career? Are you where you want to be in each area? What's working and what's not?

Identify negative messages or limited thinking. What are they? Where did they come from? How do they make you feel? To overcome the negative messages, create positive affirmations that support the kind of life you want, your assets, and what makes you a rock star.

Release the past and get unstuck. Are there situations or issues from the past that you need to release, confront, or acknowledge? What are they and how have they kept you from having what you want in your life? You can find effective releases by journaling, writing a forgiveness letter, or by having a conversation with the person you have hurt or wronged.

Do something now. Take the first step. Do something right now or today that will start you moving in the direction you want to go. Sign up for a class, pay an overdue bill, buy a journal, have a difficult conversation, or go to the gym. Just do it.

CHAPTER 3

Delish-ism

Me First.

You Second.

In That Order.

You are the number one priority in your life. Nobody else. Your partner, children, career, and family are important, but they come second to you. As Black women, we are so busy holding everything and everybody else together that there is little time to think about what it is that we want or need to be fulfilled. We are the backbones of our communities, families, and our churches. We work tirelessly to ensure that everything runs like clockwork. We give our best to everyone else and leave the scraps for ourselves.

Dominant images of Black women in society and the media include the Mammy, Big Mama, the Single Mother, and the Career Woman. The common thread running through all of these perceptions of Black women is giving: whether it is a listening ear, time, attention, love, or resources with very little expectation of anything in return. We are usually taking care of somebody else's family, doling out free advice to our own out-of-control families while cooking a big soul food dinner, struggling to raise children on our own, or are so consumed with our careers that everything else falls by the wayside. The message in all of these images is that our needs, wants, and desires don't matter.

This is a part of our culture. From a very early age, Black women are taught to serve or take care of others first. However, when we take care of our needs first, we become better partners, mothers, friends, and colleagues. And when we do not, we can become bitter, angry, resentful, or some combination of all three.

Being deliciously selfish is about putting your needs, interests, and wants first and feeling good about it. It is also about balance. There may be times in your life when other things or people will be a priority. In a deliciously selfish life, the decision to shift priorities will be something that you choose, not something that happens by default or because you are on autopilot.

To become priority number one, you have to get to know who you are at the core so when it comes time to make a big decision or change, you will make it from a place of power and control. If you have relied on a committee of family and friends to help you make important decisions in your life, it is time to strengthen the most important relationship you will ever have—the relationship with yourself.

Self-Love is the Best Love

I love me. Can you say these three words and truly mean it? Try it. Find a mirror, look yourself in the eye and say those three little words. How does it feel? Do you believe it?

Many of us spend time trying to win the love, affection, and approval of our partners, families, children, friends or colleagues without understanding that, before anyone else can love us, we must love and embrace ourselves. Without self-love, you will be pulled in a million different directions; you will accept what is less than the best from others; and you will depend on external sources for validation of your self-value or self-worth.

How do I know if I love or value myself?

Self-love is the belief that you are valuable and worthy of love, respect, abundance, and a good life. When you lack self-love or value, you allow others to treat you like a doormat or to settle for less in your life. You might abuse your body through drugs, alcohol, sex, or overeating; or self-sabotage or stay in situations that are not in your best interest or get you closer to what you want.

When you have a healthy sense of self-love or value, you take care of yourself and your needs first. What you want and your happiness are the number one priorities in your life.

Self-love begins by getting to know who you are at the core and building a solid relationship with yourself from the inside out. When you are moving from a place of self-love and value, you will be able to make decisions from a place of power and confidence. It also becomes easier to create boundaries or to say 'no' when something does not benefit you. You determine what is acceptable or unacceptable behavior or treatment from others. Such determination allows you to tap into your own power and strength when faced with challenges and adversity.

Loving Yourself to the Core

Many of us are surface self-lovers. This means that we love the surface of ourselves—and basically know what we like, what we don't like, what makes up upset, etc.—but we fail to dive below the surface of our selves to really get at the core, to what is meaningful and true for us as individuals. Needless to say, surface self-love can only get us so far. It's only enough to avoid major disasters, meltdowns, or to maintain the status quo. It's superficial. In order to live a deliciously selfish life, you will have to love yourself to the core.

An iceberg is a perfect illustration of the difference between loving yourself on the surface versus loving yourself to the core. An iceberg is enormous. In the ocean and above the water, only the tip, or about 10 percent, of the iceberg is visible. The other 90 percent is underwater. That 90 percent, the part you cannot see, is what sank the Titanic and that is what I am calling *the core*.

The surface is the things people notice about you when they first meet you. It's your clothing, your hair, your outward personality, and your attitude. The core is deeper inside of you. Other people may or may not see it just by looking at you. The core is the part of you that holds your deepest desires, wants, fears, hurts, and disappointments. It also holds the truth of who you are.

Many of us spend a lot of time making sure our surface-self is together with very little time spent understanding our core or who we are beyond the surface. When your surface and core are out of whack, although you might look good on the outside, you will fear your innermost self being exposed or others finding out about the "real" you.

When you love, understand, and embrace who you are at the core, you won't have to fake it. You won't feel compelled to buy or do things to compensate for feelings of lack or inadequacy. You will feel good in your own skin, embrace all of who you are, and become more confident in the decisions you make and the direction of your life.

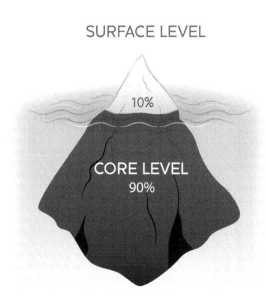

SURFACE LEVEL

10%

CORE LEVEL
90%

EXTERNAL
- CONSCIOUS
- ATTITUDE
- PERSONALITY
- MATERIAL
- APPEARANCE
  (Clothing, Hair, Body)

INTERNAL
- SUBCONSCIOUS
- FEARS
- DOUBTS
- PAST EXPERIENCES OF
  PAIN OR TRAUMA
- DEEPEST HOPES AND
  DESIRES
- DISAPPOINTMENTS

Give to You

If you have trouble putting you first, more than likely you also find it difficult to give to yourself as well. Giving to you first might seem frivolous, indulgent, or unnecessary. To be deliciously selfish, you have to learn to give to yourself and take the best of what's out there for you. The more you delay in giving to yourself, the more difficult it will be to have what you want in your life. There is no one more deserving of that promotion, that salary, that car, that partner, that vacation, or that new home than you.

Many women wait for permission or validation from others before giving to themselves, mostly because we are afraid to step on anyone's toes or of being labeled a *Bitch*. We also wait for others to give to us. Don't wait! Give to yourself.

Giving to you is about demonstrating self-love and giving yourself permission to want what you want without guilt, fear, or needless justification.

> **I feel uncomfortable doing or giving to myself. How can I get over that feeling?**
>
> If you have never done it before, giving to yourself or asking for what you want will feel uncomfortable in the beginning. You might be afraid that you are asking for too much or that others in your life will judge you or say no. To increase your comfort level with giving to you, start small and build. For example, when you go shopping, pick up one thing that's just for you or start saving for a vacation to a place where you have always wanted to go. If you can't go on vacation, have a spa day where you can be pampered, even if it is only for an hour.

Make Time for You

If there are 24 hours in day or 168 hours in a week, at least 10 of those hours should be dedicated to you—no kids, no partner, and no boss. You need space and a place that is not work or home where you can rejuvenate.

Making time for yourself can include carving out time in your week for personal grooming and upkeep like going to the gym or getting a pedicure; going on vacation or out to dinner; going dancing or to a movie with friends or alone; or joining a group based on your hobbies or interests. A shortcut to making time for yourself is saying no to something that you really don't want to do and creating boundaries with your family and your work.

In a deliciously selfish life, making time for your wants, needs, and desires is crucial. When you take time away from the daily grind to do something that makes you happy, you will feel rejuvenated and more focused.

All Work and No Play is No Good

Creating balance is a necessity in a deliciously selfish life. Everyday there are so many things to get done or competing for our attention. In general, no one area in your life should take up or consume significantly more time than the others. For example, working 60 hours a week to meet a pressing deadline or to get that big promotion is fine. However, working 60 hours or more as the rule, rather than the exception will lead to burn out and the other parts of your life will suffer.

Ideally, if there are four major parts of your life—work, family, relationships and spirituality—no one part should consistently take up more than 50 percent of your time. If you are feeling overworked, take time out to have fun. Hang out with your friends, go to yoga, or go dancing. This break or re-balancing will help you to become more focused at work or in the other areas of your life that are equally important.

Boundaries are your friend. A huge part of creating balance is setting clear boundaries and being able to say no to things or situations that are competing for your time and attention. The purpose of boundaries is to create space between what you want and what others want for or from you. It is another way of taking care of your needs first and ensuring that what you want gets prioritized.

No is the New YES in a Delicious Life

Get used to saying 'no.' Saying 'no' to things that don't benefit you or serve your best interest gets you closer to living the life you desire. When you say 'no' to something, you are almost always saying 'yes' to something else. By cutting something out of your schedule, letting something go, or saying 'no' to more work or a date you really didn't want to go on in the first place, you move closer to creating balance in your life.

We have all been in situations where we've said 'yes' to something and later regretted or resented it. In those times, we vow to never to do it again, only to find ourselves days or weeks later in a similar situation. If a situation does not feel good, bring you joy, or get you closer to the life you want, say 'no.'

In the beginning, it will be hard to say 'no' or to create boundaries where there weren't any prior. Your friends, family, partner, or boss may have come to think of your life as theirs too. They may have also gotten used to your unconditional availability or your willingness to shift everything around to accommodate their needs. Not anymore.

I try to set boundaries with my friends and family, but they don't respect them. What can I do better?

When setting and enforcing boundaries, the saying "I can show you better than I can tell," is key to getting the people in your life to take you seriously. When you begin to set boundaries or "change" the rules to make you the number one priority in your life, the people in your life will push back or resist. They are not doing this to be disrespectful of your needs, they are just used to the old you. Be consistent, use your voice, and show them that you are serious. If they still don't listen or undermine your progress, trim them back and create space for people who are supportive of your needs and what you want in your life.

Real Control is Letting Go of the Need for Control

If it is true that as Black women we have always done it all, it is also equally true that we have also probably tried to control it all. At one time or another, we've all said, *"If I don't do, it won't get done,"* or *"If I don't do it, it won't get done right."* While this might feel like you are taking responsibility or control of a situation, what you're really doing is setting yourself up for failure by not trusting the other people in your life to help or support you.

At the end of the day, there is no gold medal for doing the most or for being the most burnt out. Letting go of the need for control means releasing the grip and allowing others to help you with of some of your duties, responsibilities, and obligations.

Letting go of the need for control is also about honoring the shifts and changes in your life. Everyday, we make choices about what experiences we allow into our lives. These experiences are a direct reflection of our priorities and the things we value in our lives at any given time. To make room for the things, people, and experiences that you desire, you will have to release experiences and situations that no longer serve you.

In embracing your new experiences and the life you want, give yourself permission to release the need to know the outcome or what is coming at the end of the experience. You don't have to know or anticipate everything. Relax. Chill out.

How do I know when it's time to let something go?

It is time to let something go if the project, commitment, or relationship begins to feel like a chore or an obligation you can't get out of even though you want to. Similarly, if you no longer enjoy doing it or if it causes you stress or depletes you emotionally, it's probably time to let it go. Once you let something go, you can begin to make room for new experiences and the things you do want in your life.

In Summary

To live a deliciously selfish life, you must be willing to make you the number one priority in your life. What you want, your needs and desires come first. By taking care of your needs, you ensure that the best of what's out there in the world comes to you first, instead of settling for what's leftover.

Getting to know who you are to the core, being willing to give to yourself and to say 'no' to things, people, or situations that do not serve your best interest is also a huge part of living a deliciously selfish life. It is time to shine the spotlight on you.

KICK STARTERS AND THINGS TO TRY

Give something up. To make room for what you want, you will have to give up something and make some changes. There's no way around it. To prepare for the bigger shifts and changes you will make in your life, start small. Take a look at your daily routine and make a decision to change or cut one thing. For example, if you watch two hours of television after work to unwind, use that time to go to the gym, or attend a networking event or to do something else focused on your goals or priorities.

Do something good . . . for yourself. What can you do that's all about you today, this week, or this month? You deserve it. Start out by taking two hours out of each week to do something that is just for you or that makes you feel good. Take a cooking or yoga class; volunteer for an issue you care about; meditate or journal; or get your hair done or a pedicure. After the first week or two, add an hour. Once you begin to regularly take time out for you, it will become a habit.

Get to know your core. Knowing who you are is an essential part of having what you want. *What are your values, passions and motivations? What experiences have you had in your life that make you who you are today? Are there experiences and trauma that are holding you back from getting what you want? What have you always secretly wanted for your life based on your values and beliefs?* Get a journal; write them down. If you have trouble, enlist the help of a professional coach or therapist. You can also talk to a trusted friend or family member.

CHAPTER 4

Delish-ism

I am about 50 percent perfect,

but 100 percent real.

Flaws and All

The best part of living a deliciously selfish life is the freedom to be who you truly are, flaws and all. SO what if you're a little needy, messy, nerdy, awkward, bitchy, gossipy, lazy, indecisive, high maintenance, jealous, insecure, petty, non-committal, shy, sensitive, whiny, bossy, angry, crabby, loud, or over the top at times. The goal is not perfection; it's to be the best version of you.

Get to know your flaws and imperfections. Go ahead and make friends with them. If you don't know or understand your flaws and imperfections well, they can prevent you from having what you want. For example, if you act out every time the person you are dating talks to someone else or are always the person ruining a good time out with friends with your complaining, then you probably haven't made friends with your flaws jealous and crabby.

It's emotionally draining and a lot of hard work to pretend to be something or somebody you're not. If you're more "mean girl" than "Pollyanna," own it. If you're a big procrastinator or are always *fashionably late* to everything including the events you plan, accept it. Understanding your flaws is about building self-awareness about all of the parts of you, and not just the good parts you love to brag about. Let it all hang out.

The best thing about understanding your flaws and the imperfect parts of you, is that you will begin to learn how to keep them in check or to make necessary adjustments so that they don't get in the way of you getting what you want.

The people in your life who love you are going to love you regardless of your flaws and imperfections. They won't throw them in your face or use them to make you feel bad. And if you don't currently have people in your life who love or appreciate you unconditionally, find some that do. In creating the life that you want, you will need support, affirmation, and a close circle of friends who know *"the crazy"* about you and still accept every part of you.

Everyone says I am high maintenance and needy, but I don't think I am. What can I do to make them accept me for me?

It depends. Are you getting the results that you want in your life or is being perceived as high maintenance interfering with your personal relationships, career, or any other area of your life? If you are getting the results you want, fine, keep doing what you're doing.

When people are high-maintenance or needy it is usually because they do not feel seen or believe that their needs are being met. In order to be seen and appeased, they push harder, make more demands, and have unreasonable expectations. Instead of getting what they want, they end up pushing people away or ruining relationships.

If you are not getting the results you want, sit down with the people you love and trust and ask them why they perceive you to be high maintenance or needy. And listen. The other thing that might work is reflecting on your past including your childhood to better understand your needs and where they come from a little bit better.

Recognize the Gap
Between the Real and the Ideal

For most of us, there is a gap between who we are and who we want to be. Our ideal self is who we aspire to be versus our real self who is far more complicated and full of contradictions. For example, your ideal self might like exercising and eating right, but your real self hates the gym and loves macaroni and cheese. Your ideal self might like a partner that is nice, thoughtful, and charming, but your real self is attracted to assholes and jerks. The gap is real.

Living a deliciously selfish life entails making peace with the gap instead of trying to change or close it overnight. As we age over time, our needs and what we want shift. Similarly, when we decide to prioritize our needs and get serious about the shifts and changes we want to make in our lives, the gap between the real and ideal will begin to close on its own.

Looks *Are* Everything

Have you ever passed someone on the street and thought, he or she looks like a mess? By mess, I mean he did not put any time or effort into preparing for the day. Similarly, we have all seen someone walking down the street or into a room and thought to ourselves: *he or she is well put together.*

People who say looks don't matter are lying. They do. The way we look not only affects our confidence, but the way others perceive us as well. Personal hygiene, clothing, hair, and even our bodies send strong and clear messages about how much or little we value ourselves. And while beauty might be in the eye of the beholder, there is no doubt they way we look is an important factor in our ability to get a job, move up the career ladder and even in the partners we attract. This is not a good or bad thing; it's just true.

Looking good is not about dressing the perfect body or spending extravagant amounts of money on jewelry or clothes, it is about working what you already have and feeling comfortable in your own skin. When you feel good about or give to yourself, it will show in how you present yourself to the world.

We Are Not Born Confident

No one is born confident, not even Beyonce or Oprah. Confidence happens gradually and is the result of reaching small goals or desired results over time. It is the awareness of your power and your ability to be successful, or to have what you want in your life.

Having high self-esteem and self-value are different from having confidence. Self-esteem is how you feel about your self and confidence is the outward expression of those feelings. If you feel sure about who you are, what you bring to the table, and in your talents and abilities, the more confident you will be in your decisions, going after what you want and taking up space in your own life.

Confidence can be tricky—one day you have it, the next you don't. When we lose it, it's like, *"WTF, where did it go? It was just there a minute ago."* Even if we've done something a million times or believe we have a *lock* on being the best writer, singer, dancer, partner, mother, or hairdresser, it only takes a single look, or snarky comment or someone else to show up that also believes they've got it on *lock* to shake our confidence.

When we lose confidence in our ability to have what we want, it's usually because we have allowed fear or negative self-talk to seep into our thoughts. We also begin to compare ourselves to others or to doubt our abilities. *Am I really the best? Can I really do this? Is she . . . better, cuter, skinnier, funnier, or smarter than me?* These moments of uncertainty and comparison are normal. To regain your confidence, recall a recent accomplishment, call up a friend for a pep talk or write down all of the things that make you kick ass great. And remember, you have got this.

I have a great paying job that allows me to live quite comfortably. The problem is that I hate it and want to go back to school. My friends and family think I'm crazy. I'm so confused and don't feel confident about the decision.

You can gain confidence in your ability to go back to school by envisioning what you want your life to look like one, three, and five years down the road. If going back to school gets you closer to the life that you want, you can build your confidence by carefully planning your transition.

For example, set aside money so that you will have a financial cushion. Research programs and talk to others who have gone back to school or who are working in the field that you eventually want to go into. On the weekends or in your spare time, volunteer or intern at a company or organization focused on what you want to do. All of these things will help to build your self-confidence and put to rest any doubts that you might have.

It is important to build confidence from the inside out. We've all know people who are gorgeous, but believe they are unattractive, or people who are intelligent and underestimate their talents or abilities. It does not matter how much external validation you receive, your actions and behaviors will always reflect how you see and feel about yourself.

In going after what you want, there may be people who doubt your abilities or believe that you can't do whatever it is you want to do. However, if you don't believe you can have what you want or know that you are beautiful, talented, or worthy, the negative or limiting thinking of others, even your family or friends, can stop you from having or going after what you want.

In Summary

Being real is better than being perfect any day. Perfection is based on someone else's standards of appropriate behavior, success, beauty, and happiness. With perfection, there is a lot of pretending, ego trips, and striving to reach a goal or ideal that is always a little beyond our reach. Realness, on the other hand, is based on your unique qualities, personality traits, skills, talents, and abilities. With realness, the goal is to be the best version of you, flaws and all.

KICK STARTERS AND THINGS TO TRY

Claim your Swagger. Daily affirmations are a great way to build confidence and overcome negative and limited thinking. Affirmations are positive statements that focus on the parts of you that rock, rather than the parts you that believe are inferior or need major improvement. Make a list of your skills, abilities, talents, and the other things you like about yourself. If you have trouble making the list, ask your friends or family to help. Once you make the list, keep it close so you can pull it out in times of doubt or when you need an extra boost. Trust me, it works.

Who you fooling *boo?* Most of us are aware of the less-than-impressive parts of ourselves, even if we will never admit them to others. These less-than-impressive parts include our bad habits, such as procrastination, smoking, overspending, and our less-than-positive personality traits such as jealousy, anger, and neediness.

For starters, take one "less-than-impressive" habit that you'd like to change or shift and begin to work on it. For example, if you show up late to meetings or commitments, work to make an extra effort to be on time or early.

Do you. Don't worry about her, just do you. Stop comparing yourself to others and complaining about what's wrong with you. Focus on what's right. There's no one else better at being you than you.

CHAPTER 5

Delish-ism

Strength can only get you so far;

vulnerability takes you the rest of the way.

It is time to ditch the word strong as one of the primary ways of describing Black women. For Black women, strong has come to mean being willing to sacrifice, struggle, and take on more than our fair share of the work in our home and communities without complaint.

On the surface, it appears that we have embraced our strength or the label "Strong Black Woman." However, descriptions of Black women as angry, hostile, bossy, "overly" independent, abrasive, or defensive is proof that, although we have had to be strong for our families and communities, there is some resentment of the position we have had to occupy in order to keep things running smoothly.

To live a deliciously selfish life, you will have to ditch your inner "Strong Black Woman." Let her go. She was just holding you back anyway and creating unrealistic expectations of what's possible in a 40-hour work week.

You will also have to soften your core. Softening your core means embracing your vulnerability as well as your strength by acknowledging your fears, imperfections, and limitations. It also means admitting that you need love, support, and care from your family, community, and friends.

Get Out of Your Own Way

To get out of your own way means to take responsibility and ownership of your fears, imperfections, and the beliefs that have contributed to how you see yourself, others, and what is possible for you in your life. When you are in your own way, you can spend a significant amount of time fighting, blaming, and justifying bad behavior without any real reflection on your role in creating a particular situation or outcome.

When you are in your own way, you tend to believe that everyone is out to get you, does not want you to succeed, or disrespects your needs and desires, which in turn, makes you fight harder to been seen, heard, and respected. As a result, fighting and defensiveness become your dominant way of being. You are never at ease because you are always anticipating the next fight, argument or opportunity to assert yourself.

Getting out of your own way is about recognizing the ways in which we are self-sabotaging and work to create dramatic dilemmas in our own lives. By self-sabotaging, I mean our thoughts, feelings, and actions work against our best interests. We do things that keep us from reaching our full potential or having what we want in our lives. For example, going back to a dead-end relationship keeps us from finding one that does meet our needs or declaring you want to change careers, but failing to put in the time or effort to network or get additional training so that it can become a reality. You are the only person stopping you from having what you want.

Top 10 Self-Sabotaging Behaviors

SELF-SABOTAGING BEHAVIOR	CONSEQUENCE
Procrastination	You never get started and become stuck in your current reality and circumstances.
Over-eating, drinking, or "sexing"	You don't feel good about yourself or regret the way you treated your body. People will begin to distance themselves from you or you will begin to attract people into your life that support or encourage these behaviors.
Indecisiveness or taking too long to make decisions	You become paralyzed by the fear of making the wrong choice or decision. You never get started.
Taking on too many things at once	You become overwhelmed, burnt out, or resentful. The quality of projects or tasks suffer.
Minimizing problems in relationships, job, or health	Things get worse and start to impact other areas of your life. The problem becomes bigger.
Taking things too personally	There is always conflict and something to prove or correct. People distance themselves from you or are afraid to disagree with you.
Starting projects or tasks designed to get you closer to what you want, then you don't finish them	Loss of self-confidence in your ability to succeed or complete a project. Loss of faith in your ability to follow-through or make things happens by others.
Uncontrollable anger or hot-temperedness	Loss of meaningful relationships, jobs, or credibility.
Over-spending	Stress and continued worry about money and finances. Decrease in self-esteem and a strain on relationships.
Lying to cover up for mistakes or to make yourself look or feel better	Loss of trust and credibility. People will not believe anything you say or you will have to work extra hard to re-establish trust.

Anger is Not Power(ful)

As Black women, we rarely admit when we are angry. In our effort to be strong and or not to appear weak or vulnerable, we do one of to things with feelings of anger: act out or bury it. The reasons we act out or bury anger is because we believe we won't be heard, our feelings don't matter or that being mistreated is just the way it is.

Acting out of anger occurs when we fail to face situations or people from our past that may have wronged, mistreated, denied, or taken advantage of us. Instead of channeling the anger in a healthy way, we do things that are harmful to our partners, our children, our friends, or to ourselves. Examples of acting out include using drugs, overdrinking or overeating; using sex or your body to feel emotionally connected; fighting or over involvement in other people's lives or issues; or being abusive, emotionally unavailable, or "checked out." It can also include self-sabotaging your success because you don't believe you deserve it.

Buried anger, on the other hand, occurs when rather than addressing when we have been wronged or treated poorly, we stuff it back inside of us. We literally bury the anger. We pretend that whatever bad thing happened to us doesn't matter or has a direct impact on our lives today.

Buried anger is dangerous because it can be invisible or be masked by success and achievement. To prove we are not angry, we channel our energy or focus on things that are supposed to bring us joy or make us feel better, like our careers and our families. However, deep down there's always this feeling, no matter what we do or accomplish, that something is still not quite right. Over time, unchecked anger that is buried can turn into bitterness, depression or disease.

Anger is a natural human emotion and response. I love me when I get angry or fired up. It doesn't happen often, but when it does, watch out. It lets me know that in addition to the feelings that society deems appropriate for women to have—frustration, sadness and happiness—I can also *rip you a new asshole* if I have to. And I'm okay with that.

The key to dealing with anger is to feel it, acknowledge it, and then to voice it in a constructive manner that will allow you to heal and to move on. When confronting people or situations, not everyone will see things the way that you do or agree that you have been mistreated. In these instances, as long as you are able to say your piece, release it and keep it moving.

> **My mother abandoned me when I was a baby and my grandmother raised me. Now my mother is back and wants to build a relationship. I am still very angry and don't know if I can forgive her.**
>
> You have the right to your anger and any other emotions you might feel toward your mother. In prioritizing your needs and feelings, take as much time as you need to process your feelings and to build a relationship with your mother at your own pace, if that is what you choose to do. The most important thing is to be honest about your feelings and to speak your truth. Once you are able to release those bottled up feelings, over time you will be able to release the anger and to forgive.

There are few good reasons to hold onto anger or resentment and only two great reasons to let it go: your happiness and well-being. Transform anger into power and the love you need to propel you toward the life that you want.

Let It Go

Generally speaking, very few people are satisfied after a confrontation or argument. You may have gotten your point across or perspective heard, but emotionally you feel drained or unsettled, even if you win the argument.

Living a deliciously selfish life focused on having what you want requires that you know how to pick your battles. Fighting and pettiness are a complete waste of time and energy. The decision to assert yourself in any given situation will be based on whether or not it gets you closer to what you want or how the outcome will benefit you directly.

Letting go is about distinguishing between situations where you need to be assertive in order to get what you want and situations that are a waste of time or put you further away from what you want. To be clear: being assertive at work so that you are compensated fairly, yes. Fighting over a parking space or because someone doesn't like your hair, no.

> **I like to keep it real and let people know when they've done something I don't like or appreciate.**
>
> Keeping it real is one thing; not having a filter is another. We are not always going to like the choices or decisions our friends, colleagues, or family members make. You have to know when to bite your tongue and when to offer your opinion or feedback. For example, telling a friend to dump her cheating partner is not constructive advice. Instead, asking her what she wants or how she wants to be treated is probably more helpful.
>
> If you have been wronged or mistreated, it's okay to let the person who offended you know. However, before you start waving your finger, figure out if addressing the situation will get you closer to what you want or benefit you directly.

When you learn how to pick your battles, the people in your life will take your needs and concerns more seriously. They will know you mean business. You will also free yourself to focus on the things that you do want to have in your life.

Open to Receive Love and Kindness

Compliments and appreciation feel good. Take a compliment, give a compliment, and allow the people in your life to love and appreciate you. You deserve it.

If you have been your own source, meaning that you have been the only one in your life responsible for making sure you are taken care of, opening up to receive love and kindness can be difficult. Acknowledging you need love and support may feel as if you are being needy, weak, or vulnerable. To get closer to the life and the relationships you want, you have to open up to receive love and kindness. Allow others to touch, hug, to kiss, and to love you. Take it all in.

Most women have trouble accepting compliments or accolades and we almost always find a way to minimize them by deflecting or allowing other people to take credit. The reason we do this is because we are uncomfortable with the spotlight or being noticed for our efforts.

An essential component to a creating a deliciously selfish life is allowing others to love and appreciate you. Compliments are acts of love and kindness. When someone pays you a compliment, accept it. And, if you are not being appreciated or feeling loved, it is time to let the people in your life how you want to be treated. You deserve love, appreciation, and kindness.

> When people give me compliments or tell me I did a good job on a project, I immediately downplay whatever they are complimenting about. How can I get better at accepting praise?
>
> Start out by just saying thank you. If you still feel uncomfortable, add I really appreciate your noticing my effort or I really worked hard on the project. The trick is not to minimize the compliment or praise by adding something that diminishes your efforts like "Thanks, but I got it on sale or Thanks, but it really didn't take me that long to complete the project." Accept the compliment or praise and then pay it forward by giving a compliment or showing appreciation for the people in your life.

In Summary

There is beauty in vulnerability and in opening up to our friends, families, partner, and colleagues in order to receive their love, kindness, and support. Once you open up, the less you will struggle to have your needs met, as well as to be seen and to be heard. Everything you need will flow to you with little effort.

KICK STARTERS AND THINGS TO TRY

Share the love. Give compliments or show appreciation to the people in your life. Send a friend or loved one a card of appreciation in the mail. You can also call, email, or text to let them know how valued they are in your life.

Pick at the scab. To get what you want, particularly in relationships, you might have to revisit some old wounds or painful experiences. Left unattended, these old wounds and past experiences can cause you to self-sabotage, act out, or remain stuck. You can pick at the scab by talking to friends, your partner or family; going to counseling or joining a support group; or journaling and meditating.

Admit it. Admit when you need help, support, and encouragement. A good CEO of a business is only as good as her support system. The same is true for you. By allowing others to support you, you will be free to focus on your goals and priorities as well as do a quality job.

CHAPTER 6

Delish-ism

You have to lose to win.

In the process, you'll discover

how good you really are.

Failure is everywhere and setbacks happen everyday. They are a part of life. It's far easier to recall a time when we've failed at something or have been disappointed than it is to remember times when we have gotten what we wanted. We are just wired that way.

In society, we tend to define ourselves by our successes. The American dream, for example is all about the achievement of success—home ownership, a brilliant career and great family. We also compare ourselves to others based on external measures of success based on our culture and communities. And if its true that we judge our value or self-worth based on our successes, it goes without saying that we also define ourselves based on our failings or perceived shortcomings. For example, if your success is defined by your job or your family and you get fired or divorced, you will feel sorry for or blame yourself and be unable to see the opportunity or lessons of the experience.

As author Truman Capote says, failure is the condiment that gives success its flavor. Even the most successful person can point to a time where they failed, were disappointed by an outcome, or didn't receive what they believed they deserved. It doesn't matter how many times we hit a brick wall, what matters most is how we handle the setbacks, disappointments or past painful experiences in our lives. Life's drawbacks should fuel us to do better or reach higher the next time, instead of holding us back from what we really want,

On the road to creating a deliciously selfish life, setbacks and disappointments are the motivation you need to get to the next level. When recognized as opportunities for clarity, they provide us with reflective space we need to determine what it is we really want. When you confront an obstacle or suffer a defeat, take a step back, readjust, and get back out there.

Getting On and Off the Cross

A big part of *Me First* is learning to put your needs first, including your emotional needs. It is okay to take a time out when you've been hit with a major disappointment or setback such as a breakup, job loss, death, public embarrassment, financial disaster, or any other significant event. No explanation is needed. You have the right to walk around in your pajamas, hair uncombed, talking on the phone and watching bad television, or doing whatever it is that makes you feel better. You have to give yourself the time and space to regroup.

After you have taken a break, dust yourself off and get back into the game. For example, if you have just broken up with someone, your mourning period should never last longer than the relationship. If you have lost your job, a few weeks off to update your resume and regain your confidence is enough. The longer you wait, the harder it will be and the higher the likelihood is that you will become stuck in the past.

> **I had an extremely difficult break-up two years ago and have not been on a date since then. I am afraid that I will get my heart broken again.**
>
> ---
>
> Your delay in getting back out there allows fear and the "what ifs" to set in. Yes, you could get your heart broken again. That's love and life. Chances are the first date you go on after your hiatus will not be your last. Try to focus on what you want in your next relationship or from your next partner, rather than the things that caused your last relationship to end.

You are More Than Your Pain

Some of us are invested in our pain like it is paying dividends or interest. Our pain or traumas can be the starting points for everything in our lives and the basis for what is possible in the future. We can also use our past experiences to rationalize bad behavior and stagnation.

While I worked at the shelter for abused women I also facilitated an evening support group and heard many stories of childhood abuse, trauma and neglect. The recent abuse experienced by the women was one in an unfortunate string of incidences. Working with the women, I found the major factor in whether or not they stayed in the abusive relationship or rebuilt their lives was determined, in part, by whether they saw themselves as victims or survivors of abuse. The women who saw themselves as survivors were more likely to bounce back and understand their past as a small part of their larger life experience. Conversely, the women who viewed themselves as victims tended to focus on the past and use their experiences of abuse or neglect as a barometer for what was possible for them in the future.

Anger and pain are not the keys to what will take you where you want to go, nor will they get you to your next level of success. Many of us get to where we are in life not because of our pain, but despite it. Our past painful or traumatic experiences only tell a part of the story of where we have come from and who we are. We all have had experiences that we could have done without—everything from childhood trauma to abuse to living in poverty. What gets us through the pain of the past is our ability to see something else better for ourselves and for our lives. That ability to see positive alternatives is the fuel that will take you to your next level or allow you to create the life you want.

The pain caused by a situation or an issue is never insurmountable. When we are in the midst of a crisis or an experience, it may be difficult recall a time when things were different. However, when we have distance and perspective, we almost always realize that the experience got us closer to realizing our hopes, dreams, and desires.

In a deliciously selfish life, you have to love yourself through the painful experiences of the past (and present) and embrace your ability to overcome experiences that would cause most people to crumble.

The Common Denominator: You

As Confucius says, no matter where you go, there you are. You are the common denominator in your life and in all of your experiences. While your boss, partner, friends, children, and others might play significant roles in your life, respectively, they do not determine your happiness, success, or what you can have. We often blame the people in our lives for our current situations and our perceived inability to achieve success. When we do this, we give up our power and our ability to choose differently. With very few exceptions, we have total control over our experiences and the people we allow into our lives.

If you are not getting the results that you want or are worn out, depressed, unfulfilled, or unhappy, then take a look in the mirror. The results, situations, and circumstances of your life are the result of your behavior, actions, responses, and perceptions of particular situations and circumstances.

Living a deliciously selfish life requires that you take 100 percent responsibility for your life: the good, the bad, and the ugly. You have to take responsibility for the relationships that aren't working; the crazy job forcing you to work horrendous hours; and the weight gain caused by all the stress in the same way that you take credit for all the things in your life that are going well. You (co-) created it all. As such, you are the only one that has the power to change your circumstances and to make your life how you want it to be.

In Summary

Our most valuable lessons are often the result of disappointments, setbacks, or times when we have hit an emotional brick wall and can go no farther. We have the opportunity to choose again and to choose according to the life we want and need. In a deliciously selfish life, disappointments and setbacks are the fuel that propel you to your next level and get you closer to what you want in your life.

KICK STARTERS AND THINGS TO TRY

Yes, call it a comeback. When you get hit with a major disappointment or setback, take time to reflect and to plot your comeback. Reflecting on the situation allows you to better understand your role and what you might do differently the next time around. It also allows you to gain perspective about what you want and the experiences you want to have in your life.

- **Reflect.** WTF happened. Write it down or talk to someone you trust about it who will be honest and will help you figure it out. The most important aspect of reflecting on a particular situation or issue is to be honest about your role in creating or perpetuating the situation.

- **Get Mad.** Or Sad. Or Angry. Allow yourself to feel the full range of emotions that come with a big setback or disappointment like a breakup, firing, or being passed over for a promotion. Journal about your feelings, talk about it with your friends or family, or release your negative thoughts through exercise, yoga, dancing, or some other type of physical activity. Do whatever works for you.

- **Get 20/20 about it.** Figure out what you can take away from the disappointment or setback. What are the lessons? What can you do differently the next time to achieve an improved or positively altered outcome? In the process of looking backwards, you might discover you weren't fulfilled, happy, or satisfied and, although things happened the way they did, you know you have permission to choose again and to make a different choice.

- **Reflect again.** This time the reflection is less about what happened and more about achieving clarity about what it is that you do want. Ask: What do you want in the future? How can you do things differently? What do I need to do or change in order to bring about what I want into my life?

- **Get moving.** Plot your comeback or next move. Focus on what you want and how you can get there. If you need a new job, update your resume and start to network. If you want a new relationship, start by identifying the top five qualities that you want in your next partner as well as top five "deal breakers."

CHAPTER 7

Delish-ism

There is power in knowing what you want.

Once you know, you can go get it.

What do I want **is a powerful question.** It is powerful because the focus of the question is on you, your needs, and your desires. It is the opposite of asking *what do we want or what do they want from me?* Sometimes, we ask how we can meet the needs others before figuring out what we want first. What others want or need from you is secondary and not a part of the equation until after you have had the opportunity figure out what it is that you want.

Similarly, most of us waste time and energy on what we don't want or need, rather than what it is we do want. For example, we know the type of person we don't want to date or the kind of boss we don't want to have, but it is harder to articulate or envision the partner or career we do want if we have not had them yet. If you don't know what it is you do want, it will be harder to change your current circumstances or to reach your next level of success.

Do you want to settle down or get married? Do you want to buy a house or a new car? Do you want to be financially comfortable and debt free *(don't we all)?* Do you want a new job in the same field or to change careers? Do you want a *banging* body and healthier habits? What. Do. You. Want? Say it out loud. Write it down. Own it.

Once you've figured out what you want, you have to go get it. Begin to organize your current life, habits, and behaviors so that you are in closer alignment with what you want. For example, if you want to buy a home in a year, start saving for your down payment, research neighborhoods, and make sure your credit is in good shape. If you want a beautiful body by summer and the only time you have to workout is before the sun rises, then set your alarm clock and get to it.

An essential component of living a deliciously selfish life is to know what you want and to go after it. It is about opening up to the possibilities for you and stepping outside of your comfort zone so that your life becomes a true reflection of your deepest desires and wants. You don't have to go for it all at once, but you can begin to make small changes and shifts that put you on the path to where you want to be.

What's Your Passion?

Passion is what moves you to reach for something greater. It pushes you to pursue a particular goal or direction in your life. It's the feeling you have when you are doing or pursing something that resonates with your core or higher purpose. Your passion is not a mystery. It is that thing that you've always been drawn to or interested in, even as a child. It could be singing, dancing, teaching, sports, writing, cooking, fashion, or helping others. Whatever it is, it is highly personal and a reflection of your desires and what brings you joy.

I discovered my passion for writing in the second grade while being a writer for my elementary school newspaper. After completing the edition, my teacher called me her star reporter and gave me a cookie. I was hooked.

I discovered my second passion of helping others, particularly women, the summer between my sophomore and junior years of college when I was looking for something to do and began volunteering at a battered women's shelter. The experience irrevocably changed me and my life has never been the same since.

For the most part, many of us don't spend too much time thinking about our passion or the thing that brings us joy. We are so busy doing, living, and taking care of our daily needs that figuring out our passions is a low priority. This shouldn't be the case. Your passion should be a big part of your life—*why else are you living?*

Your passions don't have to be your full-time job or career. It could be something you do as a hobby or on the side. The choice to make your passion the center or focus of your efforts or your work is completely up to you.

Just so we are clear, becoming famous and getting rich are not passions. Money and fame are the bi-products of pursuing your passion, not the things that you pursue. If money and fame are your primary motivators, then there will be very little to keep you focused or motivated.

On the road to getting what you want, there will be bumps, namely fear and doubt. However, when you move from a place of passion and commitment to what is true for you, you will almost always get what we want.

What's In It For Me?

I hate to break it to you, but you are not as selfless as you think. And neither are the rest of us. Most of us are self-centered, meaning that our primary motivation for our actions is what is in it for us. *Even if what is in it for us* is love, the return of affection, or the feeling of satisfaction that you get after helping someone, we are the ones who ultimately benefit. Moreover, what is in it for us could be a better job or a more satisfying career; stronger friendships or a loving partner; or a healthier body; or economic security.

We have all been in situations where we have looked up and have spent months or years at a job or in a relationship that hasn't gotten us closer to what we want. In fact, the relationship, job, or situation may have had the opposite effect and taken us away from what we want.

Asking *what's in in it for me,* or how a situation benefits you directly, helps you to gain perspective and clarity regarding your current circumstances. It helps you to determine what it is that you want. Are your needs getting met? Do you feel fulfilled? What is the payoff for you? Are you any closer to where you want to be?

Motivation

Beyond "what is in it for you," you have to understand your motivations for wanting what you want. If your motivations are solid and rooted in who you are at the core, then you will experience more successes in terms of getting what you want. Motivation is the reason you do what you do or take action toward a specific goal. If your reason for pursing a particular goal or action is based on someone else's desires or wants, more than likely you will fail. You might attain partial success, but it won't feel as good because it's not based on what you want.

Many of us lead a "should" life—*I should do this, or I should be doing that.* A "should" life is based on the expectations of others and the kind of life we see other people leading. We are motivated by our lack and what we perceive others to have but we are missing. A "should" life is also based on obligation rather than choice. A should life is miserable because it is shaped by comparison, obligation, competition, and feelings of inadequacy: all real motivation zappers.

Your goal is to have and create a *Me First* life. The primary motivations in a *Me First* life are your happiness and fulfillment. You are your only competition and your path to success and happiness is the only one of its kind. Your path to success and to getting what you want will look different from the next person's path. When your motivation is centered on what makes you happy or brings you joy, the more determined you will be to go out and get what you want.

In Summary

You have the right to discriminate. In articulating what you want and going after it, you will have say 'no' to some things, people, and situations. For example, if you want to get healthy, you will have to choose vegetables over cheeseburgers. If you want to obtain economic security, you will have to choose saving money over shopping (sometimes). If you prefer a *fade to cornrows,* or an office instead of a cubicle, let it be known. The takeaway is that once you decide what you want, your choices and decisions should reflect your preferences and get you closer to your goals.

KICK STARTERS AND THINGS TO TRY

Taste and try out everything. What makes life so great and interesting is that there are so many options and directions you can undertake. From cars to careers to partners to what city to live in, the chances for variety and exploration are nearly endless. To figure out what you like and what you want, you will have to try out, try on, and taste everything. Most of us do this unconsciously, but when you are deliberate about it, you give yourself permission to own your likes and dislikes.

What do you want? In the four areas that matter most: relationships, health, career, and finances, write down what you want or what success looks like for you. You can start by making a list of how your life would look or be if you had success in those four areas. Once you've made the list, go back and fill in the details.

EXAMPLE: RELATIONSHIPS

The List:

✓ I want a loving and generous partner
✓ I want a better relationship with my mother
✓ I want to spend more time with my friends

FILLING IN THE LIST:

I want a loving and generous partner

- Make my top-five list (5 must-have qualities and 5 deal breakers)
- Go on at least one date a week
- Attend at least one mixer or event to meet new people per month.
- Get to know the person before I have sex with them
- Be honest about my needs, where I am in my life, and what I want in a relationship from the beginning
- Date the person for at least three months before I commit to a relationship
- Be honest if the person does not meet my standards or if red flags arise
- Get out of my head and have a good time

CHAPTER 8

Delish-ism

There is no substitution for high standards:

either you have them or you don't.

You set the standard for what you can have and what is possible in your life. If your job stinks or if your partner is jerk, then the expectations of what you deserve and can have in your life are lower than what they should be. When you expect more from the people and situations in your life, you get more. No one becomes successful or gets what they want by having low expectations.

Having high standards should not be confused with being demanding. Being demanding is when you require or have standards for others that you do not have for yourself. Having high expectations is raising the bar in terms of the quality of the experiences and people you have in your life. You not only have a standard for people and relationships in your life, but for yourself as well.

Setting Your Standards

Your standards should be all about you. They should be reflective of the life you want for yourself as opposed to the life others think you should be leading. What you want might not be the same as what other people want for you. And that's okay as long as you are clear about what it is you really want.

To clearly formulate your current standards, take stock of your relationships, your bank account, your career, and your health. Did your assessments cause your nose to turn up? If so, then it is time to reset your expectations based on the life you want. Make a list or start to think about how you want things to look or be in your life.

Many of us behave as though the people in our lives are mind readers or know exactly what we want and expect from them—they don't. Truth be told, without letting others know what you want, most people will fail to meet our needs and expectations. When this happens, we get all up in our feelings or upset—*How could they not know I had a horrible, no good, very bad day at work and am in need of a little extra TLC?*

A big part of setting your standards and getting what you want is letting the people in your life know what you expect of them. For example, if you want a partner who spoils you or a boss who appreciates you, let it be known through your actions and words. By clearly expressing your needs and desires, your friends, family, colleagues, and partner will be able to meet your expectations more easily and to support you. It will also allow them to share in your hopes and dreams.

How High Is Your Bar?

We all have a bar. How high or low it's set is shaped by our expectations, past experiences, our feelings of self-worth and value, and our beliefs about what we deserve or what we can have in our lives. Many of us don't know how low our bar is set until we have an experience that shows us what's missing or what we could have if we just set our bar a little higher.

For example, if you find out your inexperienced colleague is making double the pay that you earn or that your boo has forgotten Valentine's day again and you have to listen to your girlfriend gush about how her boo went all out for the third year in a row. After you get past the *"WTF, what am I doing wrong?"* feeling, you begin to realize the bar for what you want or deserve in your life is set too low. Now what?

Raising your bar or expectations doesn't happen overnight. You have to allow yourself time to become comfortable with the idea of wanting more in your life and changing old habits. The perfect metaphor for raising the bar is a track and field high jumper. When the jumper starts out, the bar is set low, but once she becomes more confident and successful, the bar is raised. The same is true for you. Once you succeed in making small changes in your life, you will become more confident and more willing to make bigger changes and larger leaps.

Channeling Your Inner "White Boy" and Getting What You Deserve

You can earn something or you can deserve something. Most of us believe in order to have the life we want, we have to earn it. We feel we must hustle, sacrifice, and eat beans from a can. WRONG! We've all known people who work hard and never get promoted or always seem to be struggling. Similarly, we all know people who get everything they want with little effort, including a great partner, beautiful house, expensive car, and bright career.

As Black women, we feel entitled to very little. Entitlement, the right to have something without much work or effort, is usually reserved for white men. And if we don't get what we want, we figure it is because we're not trying hard enough, and if we only wait patiently our time will come. Enough with that nonsense! The time is now.

I am a really hard worker, but I've been passed over for a promotion two times in the last year. I feel like quitting.

You could quit or you could ask your boss what it will take for you to get promoted the next time a position becomes available. If you have not received a performance evaluation, ask for one. This will provide you with the intelligence you need to position yourself in order to advance.

If you haven't done so already, let your boss know that you would like to be considered for the next promotion that becomes available and let her know the reasons why you believe you are qualified for the job. Lastly, don't forget to toot your own horn and take credit for your accomplishments.

Effort and hard work matter, but you also have to believe that you deserve or are entitled to have what you want. You have to know that you have the right to that promotion or corner office, great partner, house, car, or whatever else it is that you want.

Release the Fear of Success

The fear of success is equally as powerful as the fear of failure. While most people readily admit when they are afraid of failing, very few of us ever admit to being afraid of succeeding. The fear of success is related to how we believe our success will impact others in our lives: will they be happy for us or will they be jealous and envious? It's also related to what we believe we deserve or can have in our lives. If we don't believe we are entitled to success, when we get closer to achieving what we want, we can subvert ourselves and undo our progress.

Showing up late to an important meeting or declining an invitation to an event where you will be able to advance your career, picking an argument or being critical on a first date or refusing to take constructive criticism or advice are are a few examples of self-sabotaging behavior that can keep you from obtaining what you want.

In Summary

You get what you expect, not necessarily what you earn. When you know what you want and operate from that space, you will be able to create standards and expectations that are in alignment with those desires. It takes time to set or raise your standards and you may get pushback from people in your life, but in order to live a delicious life, your standards have to be non-negotiable.

KICK STARTERS AND THINGS TO TRY

Ask for more. Just do it. Most of us are afraid to ask for more because we fear we won't get it. The truth is, when we ask, we almost always get what we want. We might not get it all at once, but once we've put our needs out there, people will respond.

Expect more. We teach the people in our lives how to treat us through our actions and behaviors. If we allow people to walk all over us, be disrespectful, or to take us for granted, chances are they will do it over and over again. When we treat ourselves with love and respect, so will the people in all areas of our lives.

Speak up so people can hear you. To get what you want and to familiarize people with your expectations, you have to speak up and let your needs, desires, and boundaries be known. If you have trouble speaking up or expressing your needs, write them down and have practice conversations with a trusted friend or family member.

Take up space. Most women try to take up as little space possible in a room, at work or in social settings. We believe that by taking up space or attracting attention to ourselves, people will judge us as arrogant, overly ambitious, or over the top. You have the right to be seen. Assert your needs and toot your own horn.

CHAPTER 9

Delish-ism

If you can't see it,

you can't have it.

Your current life and circumstances are a reflection of four things: (1) the expectations of what you can have, do, or be; (2) your habits; (3) your choices; and (4) your responses to situations. If you are not living the life you desire or getting the results you want, chances are changes need to be made in one or more of these four areas. In creating a deliciously selfish life, you must be mindful of how each of these four parts shape and create your life.

What Can I Have?

You can have whatever you want. Really. You just have to believe that it is possible and have the guts to make the changes and shifts necessary to make what you want a reality. The life you are leading today does not have to be the life you are living tomorrow, next month, or next year.

The biggest hurdles to raising the expectation of what we can have in our lives are our thoughts and beliefs about what's possible. If your thoughts are negative or immediately go to the reasons why you can't have what you want rather than why you can, the chances of you acquiring your desires are slim.

Can you have a six-figure salary? YES. Can you go on a nice vacation? YES. Can you switch careers? YES. Can you lose twenty pounds? YES. Can you get married? YES. Can you move across the country? YES.

The reason the answer is YES to all of these questions is because you don't need permission to do or go after anything you want in your life. You are the *"Mother, may I"* of your life. You are in control.

I've had my same set of friends since childhood and we're all pretty much stuck. Whenever I try to do something different, they criticize me or say it won't work.

Our current lives, including the people in them, are a reflection of our past thoughts, choices, and experiences. On the road to getting what you want, you have to become comfortable with the idea of wanting more for your life and begin to embrace it. Your friends are not trying to be hurtful or dismissive; they may not be able to see beyond their current circumstances or conditions. Your job is to not internalize their judgment or criticism and to keep it moving.

In the deliciously selfish life, there is no judgment for wanting what you want. It doesn't matter. Go back to your motivations and passions. The life that you imagine for yourself is based on your desires and your needs and what will bring you joy and happiness, not the projections or fantasies of others of what you should have, do, or be.

You are the only person that can make the decision to have whatever it is you want in your life: no one else. You have to believe that it is possible. And once you make the decision to have it and believe that it's possible, whatever it is—to lose weight, get a new job, quit smoking, or find a new partner—you just have to go for it.

Your Habits Say a Lot

Your habits—the actions and behaviors you do everyday—can tell you a lot about whether or not you are putting yourself first or moving in the right direction in your life.

Do you show up late to work everyday or turn in projects tardily? If so, it's very likely that you won't be getting promoted any time soon. Do you sit on the couch after work eating fast food and watching TMZ every night? If you do, you probably won't be reaching your fitness goals in the near future. It's not rocket science. To get what you want, you have to make sure your habits are in alignment with what it is you are hoping to achieve or accomplish.

What makes some habits hard to break is that they are learned from an early age. They are done so regularly and subconsciously that they become coping mechanisms and a part of our daily routine. For example, our dietary or financial habits are passed down from our parents and families. As such, making changes or shifts might require learning how to do things differently, such as learning to cook more healthfully or taking a class on financial management.

To break or change a bad habit for good, you have to go cold turkey. No negotiating with yourself. Be strong. For example, if you overspend or are an unconscious spender (like moi), create a budget that sets limits on what you can spend on miscellaneous items and stick to it. Carry around a small notepad and write down every purchase you make. I did this once and it blew my mind. The key is to become aware of your less-than-impressive habits and then to make a commitment to changing them so that they align with what you want.

Eeny, Meeny, Miney, Mo: Your Choices Matter

Are your choices getting you closer to what you want, or are they pulling you further away?

As I stated in a previous chapter, our lives are the sum of our choices. Some choices are small while others have the power to change the trajectory of our lives. In living a deliciously selfish life, the goal is not to make any bad choices or decisions, but to make smarter choices, ones that are more in sync with what you want and who you want to be.

We make choices from one of two places: fear or love. It's true. Every choice we've ever made boils down to those two feelings. When we leave a dead-end job, tell a no-good jerk to lose our number, or stand up for what we want, we are living from a space of self-love and appreciation.

Conversely, when we make choices out of fear, it is because we can't imagine the possibilities or alternatives for our lives. We are afraid we'll be rejected or will fail. We are afraid we will not get our needs met or that we will end up alone. When we choose to stay in a dead-end job, bad relationship, or on emotional autopilot, it is because of our fear of change and how others will perceive or react to our choices.

Even during times when you feel out of control or disempowered, you are in total control of your life and choices. You can always choose again and choose differently.

Your Responses Matter

How we respond to difficult situations, transitions, and changes in our lives is probably the single most important factor in whether or not we will get what we want or reach our desired goals. In fact, every outcome we experience, positive or negative, is the result of our response to a particular situation in our lives.

Our past experiences, our families and upbringing, and even our culture shape our responses to situations. In working to have what you want in your life, you will have to figure out if your responses to situations are helping or hindering your progress. For example, if you grew up in a home where disagreements were handled with loud arguments and fights, then you might respond similarly when faced with disagreement and confrontation. Likewise, if you grew up in a home where problems got swept under the rug or confrontations were considered bad, emotionally charged situations might make you uncomfortable.

You can learn new coping mechanisms and responses to situations by paying attention to your feelings in the moment and your knee-jerk reactions. In moments when you feel your blood boiling and a less-than-flattering response coming on, step away or take a time out.

In your responses, try to think long-term, beyond your current circumstances and remain focused on what you want. In living a deliciously selfish life, adaptability and your ability to keep things in perspective are keys to getting what you want, overcoming challenging situations, and dealing with change. When you keep things in perspective, you are able to move more smoothly through difficulties and come up with a new game plan more quickly.

In Summary

You don't need permission to have the life you want. You don't need the perfect training or education, an overflowing bank account or the approval of all of your friends and family. You just have to go out there and get what you want. Once you start moving and make choices that get you closer to where it is you want to be, everything will begin to fall into place.

KICK STARTERS AND THINGS TO TRY

Be a copycat: There's no need to re-invent the wheel. If you want to make a change or shift in your life, find someone who's already done it. Most people love to give advice or tell their story of how they got to where they are. Ask questions and listen. You might not be able to use all of the advice, but you will definitely get some kernels that you can apply to your situation.

Keep a response journal. To figure out how your responses impact your daily life and choices, write them down for one week. When you feel yourself getting upset, annoyed, angry, happy, emotional, scared, or frustrated, write it down. Describe the situation in detail, the key players, and why you responded the way that you did. Also, observe whether or not a different response would have been more appropriate or got you closer to the outcome that you wanted.

Choose differently. Soon you will be faced with another choice. Instead of choosing your go-to-response, make a different choice. For example, if you normally have drinks after work with colleagues, take a yoga class, go to the gym, or join a book club. If you always say no to help at work because you don't want to appear overwhelmed, accept help.

CHAPTER 10

I am the beginning and the end.

No Need for Hot Coals or Evil Dragons

You don't have to walk across hot coals or slay evil dragons to get what you want; you just have to get moving and take action. To have what you want, you must begin to make choices and take the necessary steps that will get you closer to where it is you want to be.

To have the relationship you want, you have to be willing to put yourself out there, to go on dates and to try new things. If you want a new job or a different career, you have to update your resume, do interviews, and make sure you have the right education and training. If you want to write a book, become a rapper or actor, or an award winning chef, you will have to put in the work. There are no shortcuts or secret formulas.

When we fail to reach our goals or to get what we want, it is not because what we want is too big or ambitious, it is because we don't get moving. In our lives, the hot coals and evil dragons are our past experiences and disappointments, our negative self-esteems and our fears of failure.

Through negative self-talk, we convince ourselves of the impossibility of attaining our goals. We delude ourselves into thinking that we cannot change. We also find numerous examples and people who will affirm that what we want is impossible. We are negatively reinforced. As a result, our big ideas and desires get squashed before they ever have the opportunity to see the light of day.

In living a deliciously selfish life, you have to allow yourself to want what you want. If you want a better job, more money, a bigger house, or a loving partner, own it without apology. So what if it's not what other people want or think you should have. Once you allow yourself to want what you want and to disconnect what you want in the future from your past or current circumstances, *you will be on fire*. The fear of not having what you want will be replaced by the drive to go out there and get it.

The Hot Shitty Mess of Change

No one said it was going to be easy. Change can be a *hot shitty mess*. When a person or situation is a HSM it means that it is in such disarray or so bad that it stinks beyond compare. When going after you want or making changes in your life, it will probably get worse before it gets better. You'll want to give up, go back to the way it used to be, throw your hands up and say the hell with it, or pretend you didn't want what you wanted. And that's okay. These are natural reactions.

Change can be chaotic and can turn your entire life upside down. The reason it feels so chaotic or dramatic is because you're injecting new ideas, goals, attitudes, desires, people, and experiences into your life and they may be incompatible with your current circumstances. You are also trying to figure out what goes and what gets to stay in your new life. And more than once, you will ask yourself, *"What the hell am I doing."* This is all normal.

Once you begin to make changes and go after what you want, you might also experience rejection, heartbreak, and disappointment. These are all of the things that might make you want to give up or turn back. But don't: keep on moving forward.

Embrace the HSM of change. Embrace the not knowing, the fears and the doubts, and the chaos of change because once you push through it, what's on the other side is the sweetest thing ever: it is everything you have ever wanted. In fact, you'll not only get the satisfaction of having a great story to tell about your journey and the dragons you slayed along the way, you'll also get the relationship, job, health, house, car, family, and life you want.

Don't Play Yourself

When making changes or setting goals, we can be extreme: one day we eat meat, the next we are vegan. One day, we date people who earn $15,000 a year and the next we'll settle for no less than six figure suitors.

Don't play yourself by setting unrealistic goals or making big shifts too quickly. When we are extreme or try to change overnight, we become discouraged if we don't see immediate results. You have to be honest about where you are and patient. Deep and lasting change takes time. The necessary changes or shifts essential for you to have what you want will be slow, but so very worth it.

Start off slow and build. Make gradual changes and shifts. For example, if your ultimate goal is to become healthy, be patient and allow things to unfold naturally and in a way that is healthful for you.

Clean House

Letting go of the things, people, and situations in your life that no longer serve you or get you closer to what you want is the toughest part of living a deliciously selfish life. When you start to get clear about what you want and the kind of life you want to lead, your old habits, behaviors, friends, and even hangouts might begin to feel like you've outgrown them. To become better and stronger, like the exotic snakes of India, we sometimes have to shed our old skin.

This process is not outgrowth, but growth. Make room for your new life. You wouldn't buy a new couch and then once it arrives to your apartment decide to keep the old one too. The same is true for the shifts and changes in your life. As you begin to better understand your wants, needs, and what makes you happy, you will have to make changes based on this new awareness.

Be judge-less: when cleaning house and choosing to move toward what you want, try not to judge your friends for where they are on their life's journey. You do not want them to judge you for the choices you are starting to make, so hold off on judging them. We all have our journey and what works for you might not work for them. Just do you.

Get Moving: What You Gon' Do About It?

On the playgrounds of my childhood, the question, "What you gon' do about it," was a challenge to take action or to back something up. If you were talking smack or talking about what you were going to do, this question alone was enough to inspire you to have a seat or to take action.

Underlying the inherent challenge in "what you gon' do about it," is the idea that talk is cheap unless you can back it up with action. It is also about follow-through and doing what you say you are going to do. In getting what you want, articulating your desires and setting clear goals are only a small fraction of what is required. Taking concrete action and following through on your goals is what will bring you your life's desires

> I've been talking about moving to Los Angeles for several years now, but when I begin to think about what it will take for me to move across the country and about starting over, I change my mind.
>
> Thousands of people have made big moves across the country and are thriving. You would be one more person hoping to do the same. When we put our dreams and desires in the context of those who have done what we aspire to do, we can quiet the negative self-talk and focus on the steps necessary to get us to where we want to be.
>
> Take small steps and create a plan of attack with dates and deadlines. The plan will help you to break your larger goal into smaller, more digestible goals and before you know it, you will be where you want to be.

Living a deliciously selfish life requires that you do less talking and more doing. It also requires that you take purposeful and meaningful action in your daily life to move closer to what it is that you desire. By purposeful, I mean your actions and choices are in alignment with what it is you say you want and where you want to be.

The Golden Rule on Goals

You knew it was coming, the section on goals. Every book *like* this ends with a section on setting goals. There's a reason for it. Goals are the meat and potatoes of life. And whether you've known it or not, you've set goals your entire life and have achieved many of them. For example, when you started high school, you had a goal of completing it. Guess what? You did (or you will). Before then, you may have set a goal of getting your driver's license by a certain age or learning how to play a sport well or of getting an A on a test. You did those things, too. Goals were no big deal. You breezed through one and set some more.

Somewhere between New Year's resolutions and creating work plans for our jobs, goal setting became a four-letter word riddled with anxiety and unnecessary pressure. *What if I set a goal and fail to meet it? What if I set a goal and have no idea how to tackle it? What if I'm halfway to my deadline and I've haven't even started?* Relax. When I entered high school, I didn't know Chemistry, Spanish, or Calculus, but over the course of four years, I gained the skills necessary to pass those courses to graduate and move to my next level.

Just like in high school, the golden rule on realizing larger goals is to break them down into smaller attainable goals and steps. Don't worry about what will happen in four years or the final result, focus on what you have to do today, tomorrow, or next month to get you closer to what you want. When you do this, bigger, grandiose goals are insignificant because you have a plan.

Goals are a necessary part of living a deliciously selfish life. When we fail to articulate our goals, it's becomes easier for us to put off getting starting, making changes, or taking concrete steps toward what we want. Clear goals help us to stay on course and get us from where we are to where we want to be.

In Summary

In living a deliciously selfish life, getting what you want comes down to two things: making the decision to have it and then going out and getting it. Embrace the bumps in the roads, the detours, and the HSM of change. It happens. You just have to keep moving.

KICK STARTERS AND THINGS TO TRY

Lean in and let the shit fly. Chances are, things are going to get worse before they get better as you begin to make changes and shifts in your life. Lean in by allowing the discomfort, doubts, and fears associated with the changes and shifts you are making to co-exist with the excitement and possibility of what's next. As you keep moving towards what you want, eventually the fear and doubt will fade away.

Get some focus and a plan. To get what you want in all areas of your life, you need a plan and some goals, no doubt about it. Buy a journal and write down your goals and how you plan to achieve them over the next month, year or three years. The more explicit and detailed you are about your goals, the easier it will be to execute your plan. Make adjustments along the way and stay focused.

Say yes to the life you want. Before you can have or create what you want you have to be willing to say yes to you. Rather than turning yourself down or saying no to the life you want—even if it seems impossible today, get in the habit of saying yes. *No one deserves a good life like you deserve a good life.*

THE BEGINNING AND THE END

You are the beginning and the end. Without exception, what you want starts and ends with you. And in order to have what you want you want in your life, you have to put your needs and desires first. You are the number one priority in your own life.

You deserve everything you want.

PART II

ME FIRST

A *Deliciously* Selfish take on Life

CHAPTER 11

Delish~ism

Your work should feed your passions,

nourish your spirit and <u>pay the bills.</u>

CAREER

More than 35 percent of our lives are spent working; the only activity that tops work is sleep. Everything else—spending time with family or friends; cleaning or household activities; eating and drinking and other leisure activities combined consume about 30 percent of our time. Those at the top or in demanding careers often work 70 hours or more per week and do so while driving, eating or socializing. It's unbelievable, but true.

And because work takes up some much of our lives, it's impossible to have a crazy job and an awesome life. As Dr. David Niven says, if 99.9 percent of the parts of your car are in perfect shape, a defective .1 percent that includes a flat tire or dead battery means your car can't be used. Much of your life can be healthy and in order, but if a major part isn't working well; you will not feel satisfied or happy. The truth: Crazy job. Crazy life.

Most of us, at the beginning of our work life don't give much consideration to all of the time we're going to be spending at work or building our careers. We also don't put much thought into our colleagues, our boss or our physical work environment. All we know is that being a *real* functioning adult requires a J-O-B. It's not until much later that we stop to think about whether or not the job is fulfilling, whether or not it makes us happy or if we are passionate about it.

Given the 91,250 plus hours we spend over a lifetime working, shouldn't we be doing something we love or what we want?

In a deliciously selfish life, your job or career will be a choice as opposed to something that just happens to you or that you fall into. It will be intentional and a reflection of your values, passions and the kind of life you want to have.

A Job Versus a Career

I've been working on and off beginning at the age of twelve. My first job was selling newspapers door-to-door, and since then, I've worked at a hotel and casino in Las Vegas, Nevada, as a ticket agent at the Greyhound bus station, as a waitress in a high-end restaurant, as a salesperson in a women's boutique, as an executive director of a non-profit organization, as a director in a large organization, as a college professor and as the head of a national research and policy center at a well-known university. I've started businesses, worked for others and gotten fired one good time--No, really, I was escorted out of the building.

In the beginning of my career, most of my jobs were for survival (to cover the bills, food and rent) while I obtained education and training. To get hired, I typically completed a one-page application and had a fifteen-minute interview with someone not much older than me. The biggest interview question was whether I would show up on time for my shift. I didn't consider things like my passion, salary (minimum wage was standard), health insurance, retirement benefits, my boss, colleagues or the working environment. These were jobs.

At nineteen, I began to volunteer at a shelter for abused women in Washington, DC. It was like a light bulb went off while I was sitting in the forty-hour required training in the tiny basement of the local library—*people helped other people for a living?* I could do that. I didn't even care how much it paid.

For the first time, I also had new language (racism, sexism and classism) for the experiences of the people in my community and the women in my family. I was on fire. From then on I worked hard, volunteering in every program at the shelter, and eventually became the youngest director in the organization's history. This was the beginning of my career.

Every job that I have taken or considered since then has been in service to my passion for supporting women, families and communities. And when I'm asked why I do what I do, I always have an answer.

A Career Is Something You Have; A Job is Something You Do.

Generally speaking, jobs are the things we do for survival—to pay our bills, to meet our basic needs and to take care of our families. They don't necessarily tap into our passions or deepest motivations. If you're feeling unfulfilled or stuck at work, it's probably because your current job doesn't give you what you need, let alone tap into your passions. Jobs also tend to be unrelated. For example, one day you're a waitress, the next you're a personal trainer, and the next you're a salesperson at a clothing store. The bottom line in a job is making money whether its millions or minimum wage.

A career, on the other hand, is what you do well (your skills, talents, and abilities) remixed with your passions. When all those things come together, you thrive. And while you will most certainly need money to pay your bills and meet your basic needs, the paycheck won't be your first consideration. Your sense of happiness and fulfillment will be the number one priority. In addition, a career builds over time. It involves continued learning and growth; where you start is not where you end up. If you think of your career as a ladder, each rung gets you closer to your top desire. Each one allows you to sharpen your skill set, gain experience and build confidence. There's opportunity for upward mobility, higher income and decent benefits.

With a series of jobs, however, instead of having one ladder, you have many—and none of them lead to anywhere special. It's about the task and the exchange of your labor for money. *How boring and uninspiring is that?* Yawn.

In a deliciously selfish life, what you choose to do to earn a living will take you somewhere, get you closer to your dreams and align with your purpose and passions.

It Better Be Worth It

If you're spending 35 percent of your life on one thing, it better be worth it. You don't have time to be toiling away in some dead-end job with colleagues you'd rather not run into on the street or for a boss who could care less about whether you're advancing toward your goals.

When you have an it better be worth it attitude, your work standards shift from better than nothing to what am I getting from this experience and how does it move me toward my goals and dreams? In this approach, everything changes. You will be more likely to own your power, to ask for what you want, to use projects and tasks to get you closer to where you want to be and to become more strategic in your choices.

Go Top-Less

Getting to the top is overrated. Most successful people don't have a top; they have goals, aspirations and dreams that set them on a path that will fulfill their desires. In the end, maybe they reach the top of their field or profession; but more than achievement, their motivations are based on a deeper calling, a passion.

Did Oprah Winfrey know, as a local reporter in Baltimore, that she would eventually become a billion-dollar media mogul? Probably not. What she knew was that she was passionate about connecting with people and telling their stories. She pursued her passion and reached fantastic heights that I'm not sure even she could have predicted. After twenty-five years of a successful talk show—the "top" by anyone's standard—she decided to quit and take up her next challenge of creating a network based on her values and passions. She could have continued her talk show or retired; instead she wondered what else she could do to fulfill her purpose. She's an *amazing* top-less woman.

Getting to the top, or believing you've already reached it, can limit you. It doesn't encourage you to reach past your comfort zone, to embark on your next great adventure or to step more fully into the life you want. It's okay to imagine your top or where it is you ultimately want to end up, but treat it as a place along your larger life journey—rather than the end.

Lean On Your Success

The best measure of your capability is not your past mistakes and failures, but your successes. Success usually indicates that you are maximizing your talents and skills to bring about a particular result. When planning a major career move, looking for a new job or asking for a promotion, your past successes provide clues about what strengths you should be playing up, the kind of job you should pursue and what work will make you happy. Reflecting on your successes can also help you release the fear of taking up your next challenge, stepping out of your comfort zone and going after what you want.

Have a Come to Me Moment

In your work life, having a *come to me* moment means taking a step back from the daily grind to assess your situation and to figure out if you're headed in the right direction. It requires a full head-to-toe examination, a little daydreaming and a lot of honesty. Ask questions like: *What do I do well? What can I talk about or do for hours without getting paid? If education, time or training were not a problem, what would I be doing? What would I hate doing even if I were paid a truckload of money?*

Over the course of my work life, I've had plenty of *come to me* moments. Most of them involved curling up in a tight ball underneath the covers and bawling my eyes out. Nonetheless, during these unfortunate and desperate times, stopping to gain clarity on what kind of fulfillment I needed in my work life was the push I needed to get over the hump. For example, I figured out that I hate to be micromanaged and detest quiet offices—*where the hell is everybody?*! I also figured out that I prefer to execute my own vision and set the direction of an organization, as opposed to following someone else's plan. These are all good things to know so that when I'm looking for my next gig or my next big thing, I'll hesitate before accepting a job that's misaligned with my needs or where my boss requires incremental time logs—*ugh*.

Figuring out what you do well is a critical step toward having a career that makes you happy. Those aptitudes are based on your talents, abilities and skills combined with your experiences. For example, if when you sing people applaud and give you accolades, your experience in singing confirms that you have an aptitude for it. Conversely, if you believe you're a great singer, but nobody else including your own mother agrees with you, perhaps a little self-honesty might be in order. The idea is not to discount your abilities, no matter how hidden they might be, but to encourage an honest reflection and evaluation of your skills and assets.

As important as figuring out what you do well, figuring out what you don't do well is equally valuable. Everyone has blind spots and weaknesses. Understanding them will help you narrow down the field of possibilities for your career, place yourself in work situations or environments where you will thrive and get support in areas that are challenging for you.

Everyone's an Expert, Including You

More men than women are likely to refer to themselves as an expert on a topic—any topic—including women, babies and menstruation. Women, on the other hand, may know a lot about a particular subject—even ones that they've studied for years—and never claim to be an expert in it. False modesty gets you nowhere. Claim what you know and figure out the rest.

In our work, failing to claim what we know discourages us from going after that job or promotion because it involves responsibilities and duties that we haven't done yet. It also causes us to doubt our abilities and to pass up opportunities that could advance our careers.

This is where *channeling your inner "white boy"* comes in handy. You don't have to be an expert to be good at something; you just have to be expert enough. Expert enough means knowing enough to accomplish your goals. There will always be someone who knows more about or has a different perspective on a topic. Have confidence in what you do know and the smarts to know when you need to read a book, attend a training session or ask for help.

They're Lucky to Have You

A strong sense of self-worth and your belief in your abilities is imperative if we want an amazing career and to meet our goals. It's common to question our value whenever something disastrous happens, such as getting laid off, fired, demoted or treated as if we're the most incompetent person on the planet by our colleagues. When we doubt our worth, however, we are more likely to settle for what's given to us, take on extra work or assignments without compensation and allow others to mistreat or even abuse us.

When you understand your value and what you bring to the table, no matter what happens, you will be able to regroup, learn from the experience and to keep it moving. You will also be better able negotiate a salary that is commensurate with your experience, advocate for yourself in meetings or when something goes wrong, or to go after your dream job.

If you are bringing you're A-game to a job or project, anyone should feel lucky to have you on her team. You're a winner and they know it.

Administrative Assistants Don't Become Bosses; Bosses Become Bosses.

We all have to start at the bottom of our profession; that's just the way it goes. There's a pecking order and you have to pay your dues. Getting coffee, making copies, staffing an information table, waiting for the food delivery guys at the crack of dawn before the big event, taking notes, making phone calls and doing the things nobody else wants to do is how we learn the ropes. Your attitude and approach to these responsibilities will determine if you will become a boss or remain in intern hell for the rest of your days.

To get ahead, you have to think and act like a boss. Bosses advance because they are willing to grow and learn, and other people see this quality in them. They also do whatever it takes to get the job done, focus on solutions rather than problems, see the bigger picture, take initiative and make a crisis seem like child's play.

Bosses also look good—like they're going places. In my work history, I can recall being in a meeting with a woman who desperately wanted to be the boss of our company and her shirt was inside out and on backwards—*really, lady?* And this was a normal occurrence for her. I couldn't take her seriously. The takeaway here is that even if you're not the boss yet, how you look and what you wear signals to your colleagues how much you value yourself and how they should treat you.

Give Them the Bottom Line

Negotiation is probably one of the most difficult things for women to do. It's hard because we tend to think first about what others need and the effects of what we want on the other side, rather than putting our needs and happiness first.

For example, at work when asking for a raise or for a promotion, we consider the company's bottom line (but the company will not go bankrupt if you get a raise), how our colleagues will respond (will she be upset if I get promoted and she doesn't?), claim the reason we need it is because we have to take care of other people (which might be true, but your boss doesn't care) or take on additional work and responsibilities to justify what it is we're asking for. Wrong, wrong, wrong. In negotiating, think first about what you want and how what you are asking for will benefit you and maximize your joy and happiness. Start there.

After that, give them the bottom line: the reasons you deserve the raise, promotion, transfer, telecommuting privileges or whatever else it is that you want. This not only applies to your current job, but also when you're interviewing or have an accepted an offer and negotiating your salary. The bottom line will be based on your skills, talents, abilities and what you bring to the table—not on your personal needs. If it's your current position, it should be based on your accomplishments and achievements while at the organization or company.

Work Your Jelly and Let Everyone Know About It

You could be the smartest and most talented person in your office, but if no one knows it—are you really? To build your career, you have to let your boss and colleagues know what you're up to. We've all worked in places where the most incompetent or laziest person in the office is bragging about some big accomplishment or project they just completed. And *gasp*, your boss thinks they're brilliant, too, and pats him on the back in the staff meeting. And you're like, *are you kidding me right now?*

To get ahead in your career, you have to be willing to toot your own horn and take credit when it is due. This is not about braggadocio, but about taking up space and allowing others to know and understand your contribution to your team. You can send an e-mail to your boss to let her know where you are on a project and what you've completed, you can grab her for a "side chat" and let her know what's going on, or in a meeting, take the opportunity to talk about a project you're passionate about and eager to get off of the ground. All these things make you look like a go-getter and like someone who knows her value.

Get That Paper; Stack That Cheddar

You know what's worse than being passed over for a promotion? Finding out that a colleague with less experience and little talent makes double what you earn. It's both a stab to the heart and to the pocketbook. It's not personal—or maybe it is, but that's beside the point. You get what you negotiate for, and how you negotiate is based on your self-worth and what you believe you bring to the table. If you believe in your value, skills and abilities, the more confident you will be in asking for what you want. If you don't, you'll take whatever you're offered.

In your career, your future salary is based in part on your current or past salary. If you start out underpaid and fail to negotiate a salary based on your experience, it's likely you will continue to be underpaid no matter your position or promotion.

Getting what you want is mostly about having the resources to do what you want, travel where you wish, qualify for a home mortgage or car loan, further your education, save for retirement, have an emergency fund, and every so often, take your sweetie out to a nice dinner. You deserve to be compensated fairly for your work. Yes, you might be able to live on less, but why should you have to? I'm quite certain Bill Gates and even your most recent boss demand pay equal to their abilities, talents and value to the company—and so should you.

The Truth About Reputations

In your career, your reputation is like a credit report—it follows you wherever you go. More than your resume, what your former colleagues and bosses say or think about you can help or hurt your growing career. One phone call or a casual conversation at a cocktail party could make a prospective employer go cold. If you work in a small industry where everyone knows one another, or in which people bounce from one firm to another, a bad reputation can be the kiss of death.

To build a solid reputation, you have to follow through on projects and complete tasks; do your fair share of the work and don't delegate everything to subordinates (they will remember); demonstrate your brilliance when necessary; support your colleagues and boss; stay employed longer than six months at any one job; and most important, keep your "crazy" to yourself.

If you want to become known for something within your industry, a.k.a. to create a personal brand, you should build it over the course of your career. Take classes or seek out training, find opportunities to speak at conferences and start a professional group. In no time, you will become the go-to person in your office or in your field for information about that particular topic.

Get a Plan, Already

No matter whether you want to switch careers, find a new job or advance in your current position, you can't get from where you are to where you want to be in your career without a solid plan of attack. What are your current goals? Write them down. Related to your goals, where do you want to be in one, two, and three years? Starting with these basic questions, you will begin to gain clarity on what will advance you toward your goals.

In articulating your goals, you might discover that to get to your next level you will need additional training or education; you might realize your current job or position has no room for growth or promotion; or maybe you want to enter a new field or industry altogether. The goal is to figure it out and put it in writing.

Once you have a plan, execute it. Don't waste time thinking about all your options, what you could be doing instead, or how hard it will be to get what you want. You will surely encounter your own fear, doubts and resistance—you just have to move through them and go after what you want.

The Magic of Organized Brilliance

Most incompetent people don't believe they are. It's true. Studies show that people are not good at assessing their own shortcomings. And when they do compare themselves to others who are indeed competent, they rank themselves as high or higher. What this means is that your chance of convincing your boss that he doesn't know what the hell he's doing or that you're intellectually superior to him is slim.

Career success is not necessarily about being the smartest or brightest, but about organizing and using your time wisely. When you are able to organize your time and deliver quality results on projects and tasks, you will appear brilliant to your boss and colleagues.

Winners Love Winners

Winners love other winners. The same is true for losers. Losers feel comfortable with other losers, *negativos* and underachievers. To a loser, winners are a constant reminder of failure and lack of inertia. And if you're on your way to becoming a winner who gets what she wants—*which you are*—the *negativos* and underachievers will come out of the woodwork and try to convince you that what you want is impossible. Perhaps they've been there all along, but you're just now noticing. No matter the case, you have to surround yourself with people who are going after what they want. They will serve as motivation and support. They might also have some good advice and suggestions on how to get what you want, because they've already done it.

Get on a winning team. If you don't already have winners in your life or at work, go find some. Attend a seminar or networking event or read a new book on an issue written by expert. Find a mentor or someone who can show you the ropes, help you avoid landmines and vouch for you.

In Summary

There are many different career paths we can take and jobs we can have. In living a deliciously selfish life, your job and career will be connected to who you are at the core, what brings you joy, and your passions. If you're not doing what you love, begin to take steps in the direction that will bring you closer to what it is you want to be doing. Your life's work should be worth it.

KICK STARTERS AND THINGS TO TRY

Get a Mentor. Mentors are the best. They've already been where you are and presumably are where you want to be. A mentor doesn't have to be a wise old sage; she just has to be someone willing to share her time, experience and hopefully some of her connections with you.

Take Inventory. To better understand what assets you're bringing to the table, write them down. This will help tremendously as you begin to climb your career ladder, look for a job, apply for a promotion and ask for a raise.

Take a class or workshop. To increase your market value, build your personal brand. To get ahead in your career, take a class or workshop to sharpen your skill set and build your expertise on a particular topic.

Get a coach. If you're stuck in your career, can't figure out your assets, just can't seem to get ahead or "fix" the problem yourself—call in a professional. A personal or management coach can help you to create goals and deadlines; sort through your blockages, challenges and work pitfalls (office gossip, bad attitude, not respected by colleagues or lack of follow-through); and set you on the right path.

CHAPTER 12

Delish-ism

Having a bottomless bank account is not enough

to create true prosperity—although it helps.

You must believe you deserve all of the money

and resources that flow into your life.

FINANCES

Most black women are broke. It's true. The median wealth for single black women in the U.S. is $5 compared to $41,000 for white women. And most of us have negative or zero wealth, meaning that our debts or what we owe is significantly more than our assets.

One of the reasons we have significantly less wealth and fewer assets is that compared to other groups of women, we are more likely to loan or give our money to our families and friends. In a very real sense, our money and earnings become community property. For example, from my very first job on, I have put up bail and "money on the books"; paid utility bills and for emergency car repairs; and purchased "school clothes" for relatives and sent grocery money home to California.

Culturally, I understood my role. I was the one who "made it," and I felt a combination of guilt and responsibility to my family and friends. Economically, our communities are vulnerable, and without family support, many of us would go hungry, become homeless or go without basic necessities. It wasn't until recently that I realized that although I have a responsibility to my family and community, I have an equal and more compelling responsibility to my own economic security and well-being.

Putting ourselves first in our financial matters is easier said than done, I know. Conversations about money, debt, and finances are probably the hardest to have with others, including our partners, families and friends. There's so much anxiety around money—having it, not having enough, or losing it altogether. In the US, these issues are the number one reason for divorce, and in my own experience, the cause of many family arguments and disagreements.

Becoming not only financially secure, but also financially abundant, is a huge part of living a deliciously selfish life. To get what you want, you must have a healthy relationship to money and be willing to align your habits and behaviors so that you can achieve prosperity.

What's Your Money Story?

Everyone has a money story. It's your earliest memory of money: its value and meaning in your life. From a very early age, we get messages about money from our families, society and communities. Early messages might include: *Money is hard to come by. No matter how hard you work, you will always struggle to make ends meet. Or all white people are rich and all black people are poor. We can't afford that.*

We also have experiences that shape our relationship to money. For example, hearing family members or our parents fight or argue about it might lead us to believe that money is a source of conflict. In the same way, losing your home at an early age because your family couldn't afford to pay the rent sends the message that a lack of money leads to instability.

Whether you know it or not, your money story shapes your current relationship to money, what kind of financial security you believe is possible in your life; and your money habits and behaviors.

I grew up on welfare in the days of paper food stamps. One of my most vivid money-related memories is of chasing a loose food stamp down the street in Compton on a windy day. I could have been no more than five years old. About two years later, my mother met and married a local drug dealer. For the next eleven years, until they separated, she was courted with cars, fur coats and designer clothes. We also had a nice house, plenty of food, and many other luxuries. Money flowed like water.

The big issue, besides the obvious, was that my brother and I had to keep this huge money-related secret. We couldn't talk about it out loud, not even to one another. We told our teachers that our stepfather owned his own plumbing business. Many of our friends thought we were lucky, but I felt trapped, and like we'd all be hauled off to jail at any moment.

Based on my early experiences with money, I believed a few things: (1) Money was scarce and that you had to do whatever it took to get it; (2) One minute you could have it, the next it could be gone; and (3) You didn't talk publically about having money, how you earned it or where you got it from.

Also, from observing my teenage mother struggle to take care of my brother and me and make decisions that I am sure in hindsight she regrets, I vowed to always be able to take care of myself and to not depend on anyone else for support—not even a partner.

My early money experiences continue to influence my financial behavior, attitude and habits. I still feel a tinge of guilt when I turn down a relative's request for money. I also have a karate grip on the belief that I have to be a super-duper independent woman in order to be truly financially secure. And I sometimes spend money that I don't have, believing that somehow, miraculously, it'll all work out. Most of the time it does, but the anxiety around hoping so is nerve-wracking.

I'm getting there. To move closer to the life I want, toward prosperity, I've done a lot of work—reading, journaling and talking to a personal money manager—to shift my relationship to money, but I still have a ways to go.

Start from Scratch

Studies show that men think about sex an average of thirty-four times a day, nearly double the average for women. If sex takes up this much brain time in our daily lives (I still have my doubts), money and how to get it must consume an equal amount of our time. As much as sex, we need money to meet our basic survival needs. Money is connected to almost everything we do, whether we're earning it or using it is a means to get something we want or pursue our dreams.

In American culture, money has gotten a bad rap. It's often associated with greed, dishonesty, lack, poverty or misery. As a result, we are reluctant to admit that we desire it, want more of it or that we don't have enough of it. It would be great if we were taught early on not to fear money, and that it is not a mysterious, elusive entity.

In the deliciously selfish life, money is nothing and everything at the same time. It's nothing because there are no values, good or bad, associated with money outside of the ones we assign to it. We project our early stories and experiences onto money and act as if they are true. For example, if you believe you have to work extra hard to make a decent living, then the value you are attaching to money is that it's tough to come by; that it is scarce. At work, you might burden yourself with extra responsibilities or assignments just so that you can align yourself with your beliefs about money.

Money is everything because it is often the means we use to manifest our desires in our lives. We exchange it for food, shelter, transportation, education and other necessities. When we have negative associations with money, obtaining it to cover our expenses feels like a burden.

To get what you want, you have to start from scratch. Create new money stories and experiences. Attach new, positive values to money and see it as a means rather than an end. By and large, the goal in life is not to see who can accumulate the most money, but to have the resources to pursue your passions, live the life you want, and to have the things—material or otherwise—that are important to you.

Using Money For All the Wrong Reasons

What's great about having money is that you can use it for a variety of different things. You can save it for retirement, further your education, pay rent or go on a nice vacation. It can also be used to mask our problems, insecurities, fears, guilt and depression. When we use money in this way, we tend to overspend or give money away (usually money we don't have) to make ourselves feel better or boost our sense of self-worth. In a very real way, money creates an illusion of happiness, abundance and fulfillment.

For example, at the height of giving to my family, I felt like a human ATM machine even as my own bank account was wasting away. As the requests became more ridiculous and frequent—*a hot Power Wheels car for my one-*

year-old nephew, a set of new tires—it finally hit me. My generosity wasn't about them, but about how I felt about myself.

I felt guilty for having moved across the country, leaving my family to struggle to make ends meet. When I returned home for a visit or answered the phone to fulfill a request, the giving made me feel needed and important. I was also fearful that if I refused to give, I would be labeled "uppity" or "bourgeoise." To my surprise, when I started to say no, the world didn't end and I began to create healthier relationships with my family.

A healthy financial life means dealing with any problems in your life that cause you to attach illogical values to money, overspend, neglect your financial responsibilities or accept less than what you deserve for your work and talents.

Give the Poverty Mentality the Boot

A significant part of having what you want is believing that you deserve abundance and prosperity in your life. Even though most of us say we want to be prosperous or financially secure, deep down, we don't think it's possible. We actually believe in lack more than in abundance: We don't really believe we can have more than enough money to live a comfortable and well-resourced life.

A poverty mentality is a lack mindset. We tell ourselves there is never enough money or resources to go around and to meet our basic needs. It is the notion that we will have always to have to struggle to get what we want and the belief that when things are going well, some disaster will come along to wipe out our gains. Truthfully, it's really the premise of the show *Good Times:* That poor family could never get ahead, and the actual good times were few and far between.

A poverty mentality can also affect your financial decisions and behaviors. For example, I have several friends who earn six-figure salaries who still refer to themselves as poor, bounce checks, overdraw their bank accounts, and have their electricity turned off for nonpayment (by the way, I include myself in this bunch). This happens because what we earn is not a reflection of how we feel about money.

Subconsciously, a fear of economic security and an unwillingness to accept our earning power can cause us to sabotage ourselves and undo our progress.

Relatedly, when we have a poverty mindset, we allow negative money stories to hamstring our belief in a capacity for prosperity and prevent us from making shifting our behaviors. We approach our finances with a sense of dread. We may link our self-worth to our money habits and behaviors.

To live a deliciously selfish life, you have to give the poverty mentality the boot. Begin to build a prosperity mindset. With a prosperity mindset, there is more than enough money and resources to go around. There is no competition or scarcity. Your success and prosperity don't rob resources from others. The only thing that matters is you and your belief that you can have money.

A prosperity mindset aligns your financial behaviors to your goals. You pay your bills on time, learn how to budget and see a financial counselor to get out of debt. Your willingness to make these changes is driven by the love you have for yourself, and the belief that anything is possible in your life.

Come to Grips with Your Money Habits and Behaviors

It's not our fault. Our money habits and behaviors are passed down from our parents and families. We spend money (or not), pay our bills (or not), save (or not), and budget (or not), in much the same way our parents do or did. They were our first money teachers. For example, my mother never had a bank account; she used walk-in check-cashing stands to pay her bills and stored her money in a mattress. I did the same thing until my sophomore year of college, when I became fed up with the local check-cashing service's huge service fees. I walked into the nearest bank and opened account for my hard-earned wages, wondering why I hadn't done it sooner.

If you don't learn how to budget effectively, you will overspend or run out of money between paychecks. If you don't know how to manage credit and debt, you will receive higher interest rates for loans or have poor credit. Shifting money habits requires a deliberate effort. Few of us have ever been taught how to budget, save, invest or negotiate—and expectedly, our financial lives suffer because we are too embarrassed to admit that we don't know what the *hell* we're doing in the finance department of our lives. With regard to our finances, however, what we don't know or learn can cost us thousands of dollars.

Take a Peek; Then Stare at Your Financial Picture

Many of us are afraid to face our financial decisions, mistakes and behaviors. We believe that by pretending they don't exist, they will go away. They won't. Now more than ever, our financial decisions and behaviors have a direct effect on our ability to take out a loan, get a job, rent an apartment and attract a mate. These days, nobody wants to build a life with a financial pariah.

Take a peek, and then stare at your financial picture. Start by taking a stock of your debt and running a credit report. How's it looking? Next, create a budget that not only includes what you spend, but what you earn, as well. Are you upside down? Do you have any assets: a home, a car, retirement savings, stocks or bonds? If so, good. What else is going on in your financial life? Are you being sued, receiving letters from bill collectors or getting any final warnings?

To create a more prosperous life, you need a complete and accurate picture of your current finances. You have to know where you are starting from in order to determine where it is you want to go and what changes you need to make.

Go to (Financial) Rehab

You can recover from dumb financial decisions. It just takes time, patience and a clear understanding of why you made those choices in the first place.

I purchased my first home at twenty-five, and by thirty, had purchased two more. These were very smart financial moves. At the height of the housing market and on the advice of a shady mortgage broker, I borrowed against the equity and refinanced two of the homes with interest-only loans. These moves were not so smart. After a few years of only paying the interest, my mortgage payments ballooned and I was moments away from foreclosure. Like many borrowers, I was upside down and in desperate need of a loan modification. Between bank mergers, countless phone calls and hundreds of faxed pages, it took a little over two years to clean up the mess I created by not reading the fine print.

The point is that you can always start over and make different financial choices. You can also dig yourself out of a mess. If you have racked up credit card debt, overpaid for a car or house, taken out a loan with unfavorable terms or ruined your credit by not paying your bills on time—it's time to create a plan to shift your financial reality. Take one issue at a time and work to solve it. It may take months or years, but eventually you'll get there.

Hey, Big Spender

What you spend your money on reflects your priorities. To get what you want in your life, your spending habits need to align with your dreams, desires and values. For example, if you want to purchase a home within the next year, you have to start saving for the down payment and paying down debt. If you continue to shop or eat out every night, affording the down payment for a new house in a year is unlikely. In this scenario, what you say that you want and your spending behaviors suggest are misaligned.

Many of us are unconscious spenders—we spend without much thought or planning. We are motivated by what's happening in the moment, or the instant gratification of having "it," whatever "it" is right now. When spending this way, you might find items in your closet that you forget you purchased or that you've never used or worn; or purchase things without knowing how much you're paying for things that you no longer own or use.

To better understand your money-related priorities and values, you have to become a conscious spender. Get to know where your money is going. Begin by tracking your spending for one month. At the end of the month, sit down and reflect on your spending habits and where your money goes. It's a real eye-opener. You might discover that you spend more than half of your earnings on food and socializing. You might also find that by the end of the month, you have less than $100 in the bank.

It's also okay if you discover in the process that you spend a significant amount of money on one thing—your hair, shoes, food, or hobbies. If spending on that thing brings you joy, gets you closer to the life you want to lead, or connects you to who you are at the core, it's a positive behavior. So what if it's not what others are spending their money on, or deem important.

I love, love, love stilettos—the higher the better. Two or three times a year, usually when the season changes, I splurge on a new pair of heels. It's my treat to me. You know what I will not spend money on, though? My hair. *Why, when I can do it myself?* I also hate, hate, hate sitting in the salon for hours. While many black women find comfort in catching up on the latest gossip, connecting with other women and being pampered, a trip to the beauty parlor is my own personal hell. And I refuse to pay to be tortured. There you have it: priorities and values in a nutshell.

Mind and Manage the Money You Have Well

You can earn $50,000 or $1 million and still struggle to make ends meet. And chances are, if you can mange $50,000 in income per year, you can manage a million. We've all heard or read stories about multi-millionaires (Will Smith, Toni Braxton, Mary J. Blige and M. C. Hammer, among them) who have filed for bankruptcy or mis-managed their fortunes. These stories are pretty much the same—the person wasn't minding his or her spending habits. They all overspent, overpaid and trusted others to manage their finances.

Managing the money you have well is a skill and a talent. To know how to plan for the future and for emergencies, you have to master the fundamentals of finances: budgets, interest rates and credit ratings. I believe the best money mangers in the world are single mothers. With limited income, they have to mind every dollar and be creative to both pay the bills and take the kids out for a treat once in a while.

You don't have to be a millionaire to learn how to manage your money and speak to a financial advisor. Taking a class or working with an advisor can help you to create financial goals, overcome past mistakes and conquer debt. The job of financial advisors is to help you align your current circumstances with what you want in the future.

To live deliciously selfish life, you have to know what you are working with, financially. Once you do, you can fund your dreams, passions and create the life you want.

Ready, Set Financial Goals

You will never improve your financial circumstances without clear goals and priorities. There's no way around it. To achieve your financial goals and to become financially secure, your goals should be realistic and attainable, reflect your values and priorities, and also get you closer to the life you want.

- **Break away from the herd, want what you want:** If you want to own your own business or retire early, earn more than six figures, become a millionaire, buy a home or go on your dream vacation, own it. It's your life. Pretending that you don't want something doesn't make you want it any less.

  You have the right to spend and give your money in any way that you choose. You would never stand for a stranger chastising you, guilt-ing you or telling you how to spend your money—so you shouldn't tolerate it from family, friends or even your pastor.

- **Make your goals count:** Prioritize your financial goals and make sure they reflect your passions, your desires and the kind of life you want to lead. By prioritizing your goals and putting some of them off until later—say, building an emergency fund before taking your dream vacation to Paris, you will have a better chance of achieving what matters most, first.

- **Choose wisely:** In creating your list of goals, identify things that will help you feel financially secure and happy, and get you closer to the life you want to lead. Items that might end up on this list include saving for retirement, getting out of debt or repairing your credit. Once you have your list together, rank the items in order of importance.

- **Be mindful:** Whenever you make a big purchase or a series of small purchases (outside of spending for daily needs), ask yourself: *Does this thing or experience get me closer or take me further away from my financial goals and the life that I want?* If it takes you further away, reconsider it, take it back or put it off for a later date. If it does, go for it.

Sometimes to get where you want to go you will have to invest in yourself. A new wardrobe, new car, new haircut, career coach, therapist, different apartment, overdue vacation, and more education can put you on a desirable path and improve how you feel about yourself and what's possible in your life

- **Have a little fun:** Don't deprive yourself. Your financial life shouldn't be a burden or source of aggravation. If you love going to brunch every Sunday with your girlfriends or taking a yoga class in the evenings, do it. Your financial life should feel empowering and be a part of the rest of your life. Everything has to work together.

A Cheat Sheet to Financial Prosperity

Let's cut to the chase: to live a deliciously selfish financial life, here are a few simple do's and don'ts:

DO	WHY
Create a budget	Creating a budget will help you to monitor your spending and plan for the future.
Establish an emergency fund	Most of live paycheck to paycheck and when an emergency happens, we don't have the money to cover it. Establishing an emergency fund will help you ride out financial storms and provide a sense of security.
Attend a financial literacy class or seminar	You don't have to be a millionaire to manage your money well. Learning what you don't know about managing your finances will put you in a better position to make changes confidently.
Read books or articles related to financial management	There are books and articles written on just about any financial subject you can think of, from purchasing a home to starting a small business. You can use these books to help define your financial goals.
Use credit wisely	Shit happens. If you max out your credit cards by living beyond your means, when you really need a line of credit for an emergency or to make a big purchase, you won't have access to quick funds. Also, over time, using credit wisely helps to build your credit score.
Create a will or living trust	Even if you don't currently have assets, create a will or living trust so that your survivors will not have to deal with costly court proceedings or delays.
Spend according to your priorities	You'll get what you want and become financially secure and prosperous.
Set-up auto-pay or alerts in your phone to let you know when a bill is due.	Creating a bill payment schedule allows you to manage your money and resources more effectively.
Become a conscious spender	You should know where your money is going so that you can plan and make the changes necessary to create financial life that you desire.
Donate to a worthy cause	Giving is a huge part of prosperity. Donating to a cause or organization that you care about sends the message that you believe in prosperity and that there's more than enough to go around—and you are keeping the flow going.

Negotiate your salary	You'll regret it if you don't, especially if what you earn doesn't meet your basic needs. You'll feel more confident in your talents and your abilities.
Get rid of your poverty mindset	You don't need it. It only keeps you from having what you want.
Create financial goals	You need a road map. If you want to own your own home, get out of debt or go on your dream vacation, you will need to plan and save in order to meet your goals.
Know and understand your credit score	Check your credit two times a year. If you are working to re-build or establish credit, sigh up for a credit monitoring program that will alert whenyour score drops, identity theft or you reach a targeted goal that may qualify youfor better interest rates.

DON'T	WHY
Co-sign for a loan for family members, friends or acquaintances	If someone defaults on a loan that you co-signed for, you become responsible for the balance of the loan.
Borrow more than you can comfortably afford	Borrowing more than what you can afford puts you at a higher risk for default because if you have an emergency or lose your job, you might have a harder time meeting all your financial obligations.
Pay for food or other perishable items with credit cards	Do you really want to pay interest on a steak dinner several years down the road? If you do use credit cards to pay for food or perishables, make sure to pay off the balance or the meal before your next billing cycle.
Hide from creditors or debt	Somehow they always find you. Also, the delay in settling or paying the debt will cost you in higher interest rates and weaken your credit score. The bottom line is you can pay now or be forced to pay later.
Spend more than you earn	You will never build wealth or accumulate assets. You'll also be stressed about finances and making ends meet.
Withdraw money from your retirement account	The penalties are stiff and you will need the money later on when you actually do retire.
Use pay day or title loans	The fees are super high and in the end you may wind up paying more than double the amount of the initial loan.
Pay to have your credit repaired	Paying or settling delinquent debts is the best way to repair your credit. The service is costly and the results are mixed. No matter how many promises a company makes, it cannot legally get information removed from your credit report that is accurate.

In Summary

I heart money: If money were standing right next to me, I'd give it a big hug and kiss. I'd tell it that I loved having it my life and to come back as often as it wished. And you should, too. Money is just the thing we exchange to get what we want. When you transform your relationship to money and understand your money history, it will flow to you easily and effortlessly.

KICK STARTERS AND THINGS TO TRY

Tell your money story: Start here. This is huge. In order to improve, change or to become prosperous, you have to know and understand your money story and how it influences your current behaviors and attitudes toward finances. What's your money story? How do you feel about money and finances? Do you have limited or negative beliefs about money? What are they?

Set three financial goals: To jumpstart your new financial life, set three new financial goals that will bring you closer to the life you want. The goals should be realistic and attainable.

Meet someone new: Like a financial advisor or counselor. If you're stuck financially or have a huge problem to tackle, seek out a professional's help. An objective person can provide some tough love, help you to see where you can make changes and support you by working with you to set goals and create a plan.

Take a class or read a book: These days, there are plenty of free or low-cost classes on finances or financial management. Take advantage of them. If you can't carve out the time to attend a class, read a book or download articles.

CHAPTER 13

Delish-ism

You have to feel good to do better.

HEALTH AND WELLNESS

Most of us don't think about our health and wellness until there's a problem. Our bodies work until they don't. Prayer is a last resort when all else fails and our friends are unavailable for consultation for the umpteenth time. And we don't think about how burnt out we are or stress we're under in our daily lives until things fall apart. No more.

Great mental, physical, emotional, and spiritual health are the foundation you'll need to reach your full potential, achieve your dreams and all that you desire. This is where you start. It is nearly impossible to be sick, depressed or in poor physical health and create the life you want.

Happiness for Smart Women

For a time, it was believed that happiness was a result of achievement. Before you could be happy or satisfied, you had to reach the top or obtain a certain degree of success. The basic premise is that until something BIG occurs in our lives, we won't be happy, satisfied or fulfilled. The problem with this notion is that we are always living in a holding pattern, waiting for something that we deem BIG enough to happen—a marriage proposal, a promotion, a dream job—before we give ourselves permission to be happy. This version of *getting to happy* depends heavily on external validation.

Recent studies by the American Psychological Association, however, confirm that the reverse is true: You have to be healthy and happy in order to achieve success. Happiness and the belief that we can realize our full potential come first. Healthy, happy people are more likely to seek out and undertake new goals, find the resources to overcome challenges and adversity, and attract others with similar energy and optimism. They are also more likely to have higher incomes, better relationships and stronger immune systems, and to live longer than their-less-than happy counterparts.

Black women have a long way to go in the happiness department. For some reason, we are the only group of women where one of the most commonly used adjectives to describe us is angry. I can't quite figure out if it's a racist stereotype or if there is a bit of truth in it. Honestly, it's probably a bit of both. I'm just keeping it real.

Whether we use our health status (we have higher rates of obesity, diabetes and maternal mortality rates than other women), incomes (the median salary for black women is $39,487) or relationship status (43 percent of us have never been married, compared to 20 percent of white women, and many more of us are still searching for the "one") as barometers, compared to other groups of women, we are a long way off from happy.

There's good news, though. In a deliciously selfish life, you are in charge of your happiness and well-being—no one else. You don't have to wait for something BIG to happen or for someone else to make you happy. You can give to yourself, create your own plan to bring fulfilling experiences into your life and set the bar for what you can have, do or be. In this instance, our story doesn't have to be your story.

Get Your Mind Right

Getting your mind right is another way of saying we need to understand who we are, our motivations and what we want before we make any big moves in our lives. Your state of mind and what you believe is possible are keys to creating the kind of life you want. For example, if depression, limited thinking or negativity clouds your mind, you will approach the circumstances and the people in your life with trepidation. Every experience will be filled with anxiety, and fraught with burden, chaos and drama.

To get what you want, you have to get your mind right—become centered. When you are centered, you are focused, self-confident, goal-oriented and balanced. People and experiences have a harder time getting under your skin. You are also in touch with your reality and your place in the world.

We can get knocked off balance when something disappointing happens in our lives, such as a breakup or divorce, job loss, a major fight, death of a loved one or onset of illness. During these times, we may lose sight of our goals and question what's real in our lives.

A couple of years ago, I was fired from a job that I loved. For years, I had worked to turn a small research and policy center into a national powerhouse. From the very beginning, I had a contentious relationship with my boss, as did everyone in the position before me. I didn't care; I believed that if I did a good job, I'd eventually win her approval. In the several months leading up to the day of my termination, I was a mess. I wasn't sleeping or eating and was stressed out. I definitely wasn't happy. When it was over, I felt small, insignificant and exposed. *What would everyone think? How would I make a living? How could this happen to smart, fabulous me?*

Needless to say, I was totally thrown. My self-worth and identity were deeply tied to my work. Although I had landed a new gig fairly quickly, for months I was in a foggy funk. To regain my center, I began to journal, meditate and exercise daily. Instead of going external and focusing on my current circumstances or blaming my boss, I chose to create a routine focused on rebuilding my self-confidence, reflecting on my loss and disappointment, and channeling my anger and sadness through physical activity. Going internal also provided me with the opportunity to get clear about my priorities, passions and the kind of life I wanted to lead. Hey, shit happens and when it does, take the time and space to re-center and to get your mind right.

Get Rid of the Clutter

I have a friend who is very pulled together and high-functioning. She's fantastic at her job and is the life of the party. I've known her for years, but always found it strange that I was never allowed to visit her home. Her usual answer to a possible drop-in was that she's a very private person. One day while shopping in her neighborhood, I decided to I swing by, anyway. No biggie, I thought.

When she finally let me in, I was in total shock. It was a chaotic mess. Boxes were piled high, papers and clothes were everywhere and the dishes and food in the sink had begun to attract unwanted guests. In that moment, it was difficult for me to reconcile the friend I saw every day and the one who was spending her days and nights in squalor. Shortly after, she confided to me that she was depressed and felt overwhelmed with her life.

In creating the life you want, you will have to get rid of the clutter in your life. When our minds and spaces are disorganized, it is usually an indication of an imbalance in one or more areas of our lives. You have to make room for what you want, literally and figuratively. The clutter can block the flow of new ideas, energy and experiences from entering your life.

The Role of Past Pain and Trauma in Our Lives

Something bad can happen to you and you can still grow to be happy. You can still breakthrough to the other side.

— *Mary J. Blige*

I think Mary J. Blige perfectly sums up a deliciously selfish approach to the painful experiences in our lives. The other side of pain, the breakthrough, is where our happiness lies and where our lives are lived.

Many of us have been neglected, abused and tortured by those who were supposed to care for and protect us; witnessed our family and friends snatched away from us by violence; been physically, verbally or psychologically abused; or lived in unspeakable or deplorable conditions. We all have a story of overcoming, and as you are sitting here reading these words, you survived.

In graduate school, I had a close friend who confided to me that she had been sexually abused by an uncle. Because of fear and shame, she didn't tell anyone in her family until she left for college, but no one believed her. When her grandmother passed, she inherited a small amount of money. When I inquired about what she planned to do with her windfall, she said she planned to sue her uncle for sexual assault.

In speaking with her, it was clear that she saw the lawsuit as an opportunity to hold her uncle accountable for his past behavior. During our conversation, I suggested that her tiny inheritance would be eaten up in legal fees and that the suit would probably not result in the closure she wanted or leave her vindicated. Instead, I told her she to use the money to buy a house—a place of her own where she could feel safe and secure. She did, and years later, she told me it was the best decision she ever made for herself.

We are more than the painful and traumatic experiences in our lives. Anger, guardedness, fear and skepticism toward the world keep us stuck in our pain. The decision to break through to the other side is ours.

Confronting the Big D

In the black community, we don't talk much about the Big D or mental illness. Depression is something that happens out there and not to our family members, our friends or us. We believe people who are depressed are weak, can't handle their lives or are "crazy." And because we hold these beliefs, we are less likely to seek out help or to admit when we are struggling for fear we will be judged.

As black women, we tend to avoid airing our dirty laundry. Staying in bed all day is not an option, either. Going to therapy or seeking help is not what we do. We just stuff it down and keep going. It's just the way it is. As a result, instead of depression, our less-than-impressive behaviors often get labeled as "evil," "acting out," "hostile" or "cray-cray."

According the National Association of Mental Illness, 17 to 20 million people are diagnosed with depression annually. And women and people of color suffer higher rates of depression than others because we are more likely to suppress, ignore or bury our emotions, along with past painful experiences and trauma.

In her groundbreaking book, *It Just Looks Like We're Not Hurting*, successful businesswoman and speaker Terrie Williams blows the lid off of depression in the black community. In the book, she tells her own story of living with depression and shares numerous stories of both celebrities and everyday black men and women who have "come out" about their experiences.

Signs That It's More Than Just a Bad Day

We all have days when we feel off of our game. That's normal. Most of the feelings associated with negative events in our lives are temporary. They have more meaning in the short term than they do over the long haul. With depression, however, bad days and feeling off our game are the norm. Adapted from It Just Looks Like We're Not Hurting, here are a few signs that it might be more than just a bad day.

SIGNS THAT IT'S MORE THAN JUST A BAD DAY	
Constant movement and busyness	You are always to busy. You never have time to give to yourself or take care of your needs.
Bottled up feelings and emotions	You don't talk about your feelings or past experiences of pain or trauma. You are afraid to speak about disappointments, hurts and fears. You hold on to grudges too long.
Feel invisible or that your needs don't matter	You can't or don't know how to assert your needs or ask people for what you want. You fear you will be rejected.
You constantly lie or cover up for your behavior or actions	You are afraid people will find out or see the "real you."
Overeating, drinking, "sexing" or use of drugs	Overindulgence provides you with temporary relief from the pain or the emptiness you may feel.
Lack of energy or interest in things that you used to enjoy	You have to force yourself to get out of the bed each day or you sleep during the day or through it.
Lack of concentration	Concentration, focusing or completing simple tasks becomes a chore.
Excessive weight gain and general neglect of personal appearance and hygiene	You feel less desirable and unable to put forth time and effort for daily self-maintenance.
You are checked out	Even when surrounded by people, at work or at social events, you are not present or don't know what's happening.
You are irritable, emotional, angry or hostile	You just don't feel like yourself and don't know why. You feel a lack of control over your emotions.
You'd rather stay at home in bed or on the couch	You have no interest in socializing or doing anything.
Your physical environment is cluttered or chaotic	Things are everywhere and daily chores are neglected.

SIGNS THAT IT'S MORE THAN JUST A BAD DAY	
Every new day brings anxiety or sadness	It's a chore to get out of bed in the morning due to fear of facing the world or your life.
Feelings of hopeless, desperation, or despair	You feel as if you are at your rope's end and that you can't handle one more day.
Nagging and persistent feeling that something's just not right	You just can't figure out what's going on or why you're acting the way that you are.
Lack of self-efficacy	You don't feel effective or that you can accomplish your daily tasks or goals.

Undiagnosed depression can cause us to abuse ourselves through the use drugs or alcohol; to lose interest in our work, family and our lives; or to harm loved ones or ourselves. Depression is not a temporary lack of self-motivation, but a dark cloud that makes everything you attempt to do seem like a huge effort.

To live a deliciously selfish life, we must be aware of and understand ourselves completely. And we also have to seek out help when we need it. Being healthy, present and alert is what will help invite good things into your life.

Loving our Sticks and Curves

Growing up, I had exactly zero curves. I was flat from the back and the front. While my friends blossomed, I struggled to get out of a training bra. My cousins on my father's side were Amazons in the best sense of the word—but what about me? *When would I get some meat on these bones?*

Apparently never. Even in college I was rejected by the local blood bank because my tiny 98-pound frame was considered too high risk for a donation. I wanted the typical black woman body—round hips and *plump ass—so, so bad*. No, really I prayed for it. I felt embarrassed, and as if I was missing something. To compensate, I wore extra layers of clothing and stuffed my bra with tissue. Imagine my horror when my secret was discovered while leaning over in class; a cutie looked down my shirt and saw my extra help.

As women, we learn early on what's considered an "acceptable" body from our communities and families. And our first real understanding of our bodies and how to treat them comes from our mothers and the other women in our lives. We internalize and model their treatment and attitudes toward their bodies. My mother never talked about bodies, weight or sex with me. When I got my period, to get around having "the talk," she gave me carnations and *The Miracle of Life* video. There was no question-and-answer period after the viewing. All I needed to know was in the video; no further explanation needed.

Recent studies claim that black women are happier with our bodies than other women even though we are more likely to be overweight or obese. Perhaps it's because we embrace our curves, and the people in our lives who love us do as well. I'm not sure. To be perfectly honest, I'm not completely sold on the idea that black women are "happier" with our bodies or have a more positive body image than other women. The reason this seems odd to me is that there are very few positive messages or images of black women bodies in the media and in our culture. And when they are present, our bodies are usually reduced to a piece of ass or used to peddle an album or an over-the-top lifestyle.

My theory is that we black women don't spend too much time thinking about our bodies. Like many of the other areas of our lives that get neglected when we put others first, we don't talk about weight gain or loss; exercise or our eating habits; or the abuses perpetrated against our bodies on a regular basis. And we most certainly don't talk about our bodies in relation to our happiness, self-esteem or self-worth.

As a result, we are outside of our bodies. What I mean is that we don't make the connection between the ways we treat our bodies, how we feel about ourselves and what is happening in our lives. It's all connected. When we are disconnected from our bodies, we tend to mistreat, abuse or neglect them—and by extension, our health—by overeating, overworking, putting off wellness exams and checkups, refusing to ask for help and support or allowing others to use our bodies for their pleasure.

To live a deliciously selfish life, you have to get back into your body. Live with it and treat it well. Once you become aware of your body, it'll do more than get you from A to B. It'll take you to where you want to go.

Weight Watching and Hip Consequences

We gain weight when we're stressed or make major changes in our lives; when we become pregnant or after we give birth; when we fall in or out of love; and when we go to the family reunion or on vacation. Weight fluctuation is a normal part of most women's lives. And our bodies change as we age. For example, the body I had in my twenties is not the body that I have in my thirties after having twins. And I'm okay with that. I do, however, miss eating whatever I want without hip consequences.

About four in five black women in the US are overweight or obese, and black girls are 80 percent more likely be overweight than their peers. Putting aside the fact that culturally, we prefer curves to sticks, the current rate of obesity among black women and girls is more than alarming. I love my mama's cooking, too, but this is a real problem.

Similar to our money habits and stories, our relationship to food is learned from our families. We learn what tastes good or doesn't, and how to shop, season and cook food in the comfort of our homes, usually from our mothers or grandmothers. And when we're not cooking for ourselves, we learn from our families and caregivers where to purchase food similar to those eaten at home. We're also not taught how to manage our eating through our caloric intake or how to exercise until it's too late—usually from a doctor.

It is too easy to blame our high obesity rates on collard greens, peach cobbler and Pepsi. The problem goes much deeper. It's about what we don't know or haven't been taught about food, diet and exercise; about our emotions and how we feel about our bodies and ourselves; and about putting our needs last. For example: How many times have you worked through lunch and found yourself ordering fast food because you believed you couldn't leave your desk?

Or how many times have you overeaten because you felt angry, rejected or disappointed? I bet often.

Eating right and taking care of our bodies are acts of self-love, preservation and acceptance. When we understand our personal relationship to food and connect fully with our bodies, we can begin to make choices that are reflective of who we believe ourselves to be at our core and in the world.

Migraines, Hair Loss, and Weight Gain: Pay attention, Your Body's Trying to Tell You Something

Personal growth author Louise Hay believes that we co-create every illness in our bodies. Our bodies, she says, are like everything else in our lives: mirrors of our inner thoughts and beliefs. Our bodies are always talking to us and telling us what's wrong or right in our lives—we just have to pay attention.

For example, kids and germs aside, when we come down with a severe cold, it's usually because we have exhausted ourselves and our body takes a break without us. When we gain excessive weight out of the blue, it's typically because we are refusing to deal with emotional pain, rejection, or insecurities and are using food to cope. Migraines can be attributed to stress, conflict or built up resentment in our lives that is literally eating away at us.

You can medicate, run away or try to cover up problems, but until you deal with the root causes, they won't go away and you will continue to feel their effects on your life and in your body.

That's for White People and Other Fatty Lies

Here is what I've heard: *Black people don't exercise. We aren't vegetarians. We don't diet. We don't go to therapy. We don't get depressed. We hate hiking, swimming and yoga.* Those are things white people do. That's a big fatty lie.

Believing that something, whether it's exercising or managing your finances and credit well, is white and therefore off-limits is the epitome of when *keeping it real* goes wrong. White, rich or extra-good-looking people don't have a monopoly on living well. This mentality is killing us and prevents us from reaching our full potential. Black people do all of the above and more; we just don't talk about it. To have the life you want, you have to step out of your comfort zone and be willing to try new things.

The Secret Swag Sauce to Getting What You Want

I would be less than forthright if I didn't share with you the real, real secret to getting what you want and to living a deliciously selfish life. Here it is: Take time and space to focus on your needs and what you want through visualization, prayer, meditation and reflection. *Ta-da.* That's it.

Carving out time to reflect and to refocus give you a chance to gain perspective on what it is that you want to attract into your life. In doing so, you'll also become more attuned to what is keeping you from what you desire.

Visualization is the process of imagining what you want in your life before you actually have it. Before I ever knew what visualization was, I used it to counter the negativity that surrounded me as a child and teenager. I imagined myself living a different life—one based on my dreams and desires.

In addition to imagining the life I want, I also write about it in a journal. I write down my goals and dreams and revisit them almost daily. When journaling, try not to worry about your spelling and grammar or judge what comes out. Just do it. I love going back weeks, months or even years later and crossing something off of my list.

I didn't learn how to pray until well into my adulthood. Sure, I knew how to clasp my hands together, close my eyes and ask God for help when I had messed up or needed a miracle, but I didn't really get the purpose of prayer until much later. The purpose of prayer, I believe, is to open us up to receive the abundance and light that is available to us all from the source of all things. By light, I mean the grace and unconditional love that is available 24/7 from God.

When I pray or mediate (another form of prayer), I reflect on my desires and the blockages that prevent me from bringing what I want into my life. I also ask that I understand all that I need to know about my experiences and circumstances as I move throughout my day. That's it. Not a huge production, but it allows me to release anxiety and the fear of not knowing what's around the corner.

In a nutshell: Start your day off right—focused on your needs, what you want to accomplish and your priorities. *Nobody's day should begin with somebody else's problems, including yours.* Many of us from the time we wake up, we're consumed with someone else's problems or drama—no matter if it's our children, partner, boss or friends. Take 15 to 30 minutes to go internal and to visualize and reflect on your priorities and what it is that you want. It'll go along way.

In Summary

You have to be in good physical, emotional, mental and spiritual health to bring what you want into your life. There's no doubt about it. When you are happy, present and alert, you feel and believe that you can have it all. And you will.

KICK STARTERS AND THINGS TO TRY

Get some help. Invest in your health and well-being. If you need help getting started making shifts, have a tough issue from your past that you need help resolving or want to create a plan to get healthy, enlist the help of a professional. A therapist, life coach or support group can help move you toward what you want more quickly and identify challenges or blockages.

Make it a five-star week. Do something healthy or that's good for you for five days in a row. Go to the gym, take a class, eat a salad or go without fast food or some other indulgence for five days. Doing so builds your commitment and discipline to making larger changes in your life.

Eat brussels sprouts. Try something new. For example, I used to say that I didn't like salmon or duck, but the truth was, I had never tried either one. When I learned how to cook salmon, I loved it. The jury, however, is still out on the duck. The bottom line is: Don't say you don't like something if you've never even tried it. Give it a shot. You might just like it.

Take thirty. In a quiet place and without distractions, take thirty minutes at the beginning or end of your day to re-center and focus on your goals, priorities and desires. Pray, meditate or journal.

DISCLAIMER:

This chapter will not teach you how to get a man or

provide you with little sneaky tips to trick people into

falling in love with you.

So put your highlighter down and relax.

CHAPTER 14

Whenever you're ready,

love will seek you out.

RELATIONSHIPS

Finding love and a good relationship are such complicated subjects. Everyone has opinion on what we should do to find the one: *Act like a lady, think like a man; be submissive and let him think he's in charge; put it down in bed and in the kitchen; or dumb it down because men don't like women who know or earn more than they do.* It's all so confusing. Which advice should you follow?

Lately there have been several books written by self-styled experts focused on the so-called relationship crisis among black women. You have heard about the crisis haven't you? It's the one that claims there are tons of smart, eligible black women and too few partners to go around. The ratio is 1,000 women for every man. (I'm exaggerating.) And as a result, we'll never marry and die alone comforted only by our success, cats and BFFs.

I'm calling BS on this crisis. What this alleged crisis has done is to create a scarcity mentality among women, causing us to feel bad about ourselves and to lower our standards when it comes to finding a partner. It also makes us willing to try just about anything (once) to get a partner: *The book says to do this, so I'll give it a shot.* Or *the relationship panel of Boris Kodjoe-esque-looking men say they prefer women who do this, so I'll try it.* Truthfully, the only real "expertise" these experts have is their own opinions, preferences and experiences, which may or may not apply to you. The sneaky tips and tricks may work for a while, but they are not enough to sustain a relationship or to attract someone who loves and appreciates all of who you are.

To get the relationship you want, you have to be ready to accept love into your life. You have to become vulnerable and allow yourself to want and be wanted. You also have to do the work to gain closure and heal the wounds from the past that may have caused you to sabotage relationships.

Are You Ready for Love?

You are probably nodding your head yes. Who wouldn't be? Unless you've just gotten out of a relationship with Lucifer himself, most of us believe we're ready for the next relationship to be The One. We can't wait to love and be loved completely. And who could blame us? Many of us have been dating for more than two decades.

Around sixteen, when we first begin to date, relationships aren't that complicated and our expectations are pretty low. We're not necessarily looking to have our emotional needs met, start a family, get married or split the bills. Our only real expectation is to be liked and to have fun. We get together, hook up, break up, and keep it moving.

As we get older, relationships and dating become high-stakes investments filled with tons of fear and anxiety. In what seems like a matter of minutes, we go from fun and games to looking for The One without truly having a sense of who we are and want we want out of a relationship. We say we want love, but *love* is often code for other the things we crave, such as security, validation, support, comfort and a sense of belonging.

In order to be ready for love, you have to do the internal work to become enough for you. What I mean by *enough* is that you're okay with who you are, with or without a relationship. When you believe you are enough and have taken the time to understand who you are at the core, a healthy and loving relationship will be the icing on the cake, not the thing you need to feel fulfilled.

The Real You in Relationships

Who are you in relationships? How do you behave? What do you expect? Are you fearful? Are you defensive? Are you emotionally closed? Are you getting your needs met?

Our relationship DNA—or who we are in relationships—is a reflection of our family histories, relationships with our parents or guardians, and our past dating experiences. For example, if you grew up in a cold, unloving or abusive home, in relationships you might seek out partners or co-create experiences that affirm your beliefs or expectations about relationships. Similarly, if you grew up in a home with traditional gender roles, your expectations of how you should be treated and how you should behave will be similarly shaped.

Who we are in romantic relationships is different from who we may be at work, socially or with our families. For example, you might be assertive and articulate about your needs at work, but have a hard time letting your partner know what you need or want in the relationship. To have better and more fulfilling relationship experiences, you have to figure out your relationship DNA, your patterns and why you do the things you do.

To better understand you relationship DNA, take a moment to review your past three relationship experiences. What were they like? How and why did they end? How did you feel in them? Are there common themes, messages or patterns that run through all of them? Chances are, when you rewind, the issues, patterns and behaviors that make up your relationship DNA will come to light.

Throughout my twenties and into my early thirties, I bounced from one relationship to another. I was a serial dater and heartbreaker in the worst sense of the word. I would start relationships off with great intensity and interest, nearly overwhelming the other person. After a few months of dating and sharing just about everything, I would find an excuse to end it. Some of my greatest hits include:

- You're going to the Air Force. You know I hate the military and violence. Oh, this is the first you're hearing of this? Well, it's true.

- You don't love me. You just *think* you do. How can I be with someone who can't even judge the proper length of time before you should love someone?

- You read *Time Magazine*? Who reads *Time Magazine*? It's conservative and not progressive enough. Clearly, we don't share the same core values.

- You thought we were dating? I never said that. This is not good. I'm beginning to feel smothered.

- I'm just not feeling it. I don't know why. It's me. Maybe I need to take some time to figure out what I want. When I do figure it out, I hope you'll still be available. I'll completely understand if you've moved on.

My all-time favorite, go-to strategy when I couldn't come up with an excuse was the Houdini—no call, no text, no e-mail. I just disappeared without a trace. This was probably the messiest because it involved "pop-ups" and uncomfortable encounters months down the road. A "pop-up" is when someone swings by your house unannounced just to talk. Pretending not to be home when my car was parked out front was beyond awkward.

Needless to say, I was a *hot shitty mess* when it came to relationships. What's so twisted is that during that period of life, I was convinced that *they* were the problem. Self-righteously, I would complain to my friends about all the good ones being taken (although I couldn't confirm this) and wonder how a catch like me could be perpetually single.

Years and hundreds of dollars in therapy later, I realized that it was me and not them that was the cause of the relationships' premature demise. I was the one hurting, broken and with the issues. As a result of my childhood experiences of abandonment and neglect, I didn't feel worthy of love and feared that if I opened up, I would be hurt or disappointed. So, in my relationships, I found an excuse to run whenever I began to feel vulnerable. Deep stuff, I know.

The takeaway is that our relationship DNA influences what we expect, how we behave and our responses in relationships. And unless we do the work to understand who we are in relationships or why we do the things that we do, we will continue to repeat the same patterns.

The Real Reason You're Still Single

The truth about intimate relationships is that they can never be any better than our relationships with ourselves. —James Hollis, The Middle Passage

Before you can get to *We*, you have to get to *Me*. There's no way around it. Relationship therapist and author Katharine Woodward Thomas believes our issues in relationships mirror our internal issues with ourselves. If we are having difficulty sustaining loving, nurturing and committed relationships, the place to look first is within: How are we failing to love, nurture and commit to ourselves?

This is true. It's much easier to focus on others and what they should be giving to us than to turn our attention toward what we need to give to ourselves in order to accept love into our lives. We have to love and give to ourselves first. When we are unloving, critical or hurtful to ourselves, we tend to attract people into our lives who are unloving, abusive or hurtful towards us. They confirm and reflect our beliefs about who we are. At a very deep level, we feel unworthy of love. But when we transform our self-perception and what we believe is possible in our lives, we will begin to attract people who love and appreciate us for who we are.

You can *love* yourself by taking time out to attend to your needs and desires. *Nurture* yourself by embracing all the parts of your personality and turning off the negative self-talk. You can *commit* to yourself by showing up and being present in your own life. These are all of the things that you would like a partner to reflect back to you in a relationship. Do them for yourself now.

Healing Our Wounds

We are not born emotionally closed, distrusting, or feeling unworthy and lonely; we internalize these feelings throughout our early encounters in relationships. In childhood, it doesn't take much to shape our perception of the world and the people in it. When we fail to have our needs met, are abandoned by a parent or mistreated or abused by a friend or caregiver, we absorb it into our very souls and develop coping mechanisms to deal with the pain or feelings. The scars that we carry from these past experiences are duplicated in our later, intimate relationships and affect our capacity to love and accept love from others.

When we fully understand our core wounds—the painful, traumatic experiences that shape who we are from childhood on—we can begin to make healthier decisions about relationships, establish healthier habits and patterns that are in alignment with the love we desire, and ultimately begin to heal.

Letting Go of What You Never Received

We cannot change our early experiences of neglect, abuse or trauma. And in the present moment, we cannot expect the people who enter our lives to give us what we never received. Yes, they can love us, but they will never be able to fill the void left by an absent parent or make up for the lack of love, security or attention we experienced as children.

Our less-than-impressive behaviors in relationships often have their roots in what we failed to receive or how we interpreted the behavior of our parents or caregivers towards us. For example, if your father abandoned you when you were a child, you might believe the same will happen to you in your romantic relationships. You might also have built up anger or resentment that affects your current relationships. Neediness, fear of abandonment, fear of attachment, emotional detachment, jealousy, co-dependency and anger are all the results of some unmet core need in our formative years.

To heal, you have to go straight to the source of the pain or the trauma. Until you are able to fully understand your early relationships with those entrusted to love, care and provide for you, you will never be free to create the relationship you want in your life.

You Don't Need Maury for This:
Valuing Ourselves in Relationships

Our own confidence, clarity, and healthy self-worth end up being reflected in the partners we choose. Similarly, when lack self-value or self-worth, we tolerate foolishness (cheating and lying), allow others to treat us like a doormat or accept less than what we deserve in relationships.

Even if we are strong and confident in other areas in our lives, such as our career, we may end up being treated poorly in relationships—and we can't quite wrap our heads around the discrepancy. We are unable to recognize our behavior (or even ourselves) and may rationalize poor treatment from others. And in our hearts it all makes sense even when everything around us tells us it's wrong.

Recently, one of my good friends confided to me that she had been cheated on by her partner. She discovered the infidelity on Valentine's Day—*of all days*—by finding two Valentine's cards: one addressed to her and the other to the mistress. The affair had been going on for several months. Once confronted, her partner left home for a few weeks and upon his return stated he planned to continue to stay in the house, but no longer wanted to be in the relationship. Okay, we've all been there. The kicker is that for months, she carried the financial load, covered the mortgage and the bills and shuttled him back and forth to work because he did not own a car. *Are you kidding me?*

Even when we believe it's all about the other person and their behavior toward us, it's really about us and how we feel about ourselves. When we allow others to mistreat us, or when we take on more than our fair share of the emotional and financial weight in a relationship, it is because we believe we are unworthy of love and do not deserve happiness.

You are in control of how you are treated in relationships and in your life. And what matters most are your responses and what you choose to do with the information presented to you. Do you stand up for yourself, or do shrink and accept what is being offered?

As you begin to value yourself more fully, you will feel empowered to yourself to communicate your needs and desires in relationships, leave a relationship that is unhealthy, and to recognize where your needs are not getting met. In the end, we must love ourselves more than we love the relationship and more than we fear being alone.

Who You Trying to Catch?

The better you feel about yourself the more attractive you will be to others. You won't need to be saved, rescued or "fixed." The love you have for yourself will shine through in how you carry yourself, your actions and ultimately how high you set the bar in choosing a partner. When you feel good about yourself and have done the self-work, you earn the right to be choosy.

To get the relationship that you want, you'll have to gain clarity on what is that you desire in a partner. In addition to physical attraction, you should also consider other qualities and characteristics such as personality, attitude, hobbies and interests, relationship to friends and family, educational background and financial management skills (don't overlook this or you'll be sorry). Your list might be longer, but you get my drift. The clearer you are about what you want, the better luck you will have in attracting someone who's right for you.

A word of caution: Try not to be too picky. Pickiness is the official Saturday night sponsor of loneliness. To start gaining clarity on what you want in a relationship without creating a ransom list of demands, make a list of the top five qualities you desire in a partner and the top five deal-breakers (things that you will not put up with). From there, reflect on your most recent relationships and what you found exciting or interesting about that person or relationship.

Stop Making Excuses:
Maybe You're Just Not That Into Him

Many of us believe that something catastrophic has to happen for a relationship to end—lying, cheating, drug addiction and bank robbery, among them. (I've heard all of these reasons, by the way.) It's not true, though. The best way to end a relationship is before the drama and chaos strike—at the moment you realize that you're just not that into him.

It's okay not to like him as much he likes you. And it's also okay to end it. The reason we don't end relationships when its time is because we fear not being able to find someone else. We allow our negative and limiting self-talk to keep us stuck: *What if I don't find somebody else? I'm too old to get back out there. All of the good ones are taken. I don't even know how to date anymore.* We might also feel that we will be judged by our friends and families or believe we'll regret it, later.

Ending a relationship or deciding not pursue a connection frees you up to attract the right person into your life. So what if everyone thinks he's amazing? You don't. And that's all that matters. In all areas of your life, give yourself permission to want what you want.

Don't Look Back

When you end it, end it. Don't look back. Going back to a relationship that wasn't working is like going back to a job you've been fired from the next day. You crave the security, but know deep down it wasn't a good fit for each of you. Yes, heartbreak is painful and getting dumped sucks, but it's only temporary. The truth is ole whatshisname won't matter in the grand scheme of your fabulous life—not in a few months, and definitely not a year from now. Holding on to a sour, no-good relationship keeps you from getting the relationship you actually do want. And who has time for that?

Admit You Need It

Just admit it. You need love. It doesn't matter if you are five or fifty-five; we all have a desire to be loved, nurtured and supported. Career success and riches are great, but without love and meaningful connection, what does wealth really matter? Coming home to an empty mansion is no fun. Sharing and building a life with someone feels good, and we all deserve to experience that kind of goodness at least once—hopefully many times over—in our lives.

We are taught to be independent. This is especially true of black women. We learn from a very early age how to meet our own needs and sustain ourselves mentally and emotionally. As a result, when it's time to open up or depend on a partner, we are fearful and reluctant. We also don't trust what might happen if we do. *Will I be rejected? Will I lose face? Will I be able to pull myself back together again?* We also believe vulnerability always leads to pain and hurt.

A willingness to be open and vulnerable is a key to attracting love and later, sustaining a fulfilling relationship. By vulnerable, I mean taking the risk to feel deeply, express your needs, speak your truth, cry and ask for what you want. One of my favorite sayings is, "Love like you'll never be hurt." What this means is that we are not fearful of repeating our past, painful relationships, and instead live in the present moment. Our pasts cannot touch us or do us harm. It also means that we accept the risk associated with love and understand that we might get hurt. Give it a try.

A Man Versus a Partner

Anybody can get a man. I truly believe this. To get the life you want, however, you'll need a partner. A partner is someone who is committed to your happiness, personal growth and success. They don't mind a 50–50 partnership or an 80–20 split (in your favor) at times, because they know that's what it takes to build a life with someone. They're also not threatened or intimidated by your ambition, income or intelligence; your shine is their shine, too. Ursula Burns, head of Xerox and the only African American woman serving as CEO in the Fortune 500 attributes her success, in part, to having a supportive (and elder) partner who is as committed to her success as she is.

Partners see all sides of you—the good, the bad, and the ugly—and still stick around. They know your flaws, secrets and fears and reflect back to you the best of who you are, especially those times you're knee-deep in doubt. And above all, a partner wants to be there with you and makes it known through their words, actions and behaviors.

Opening up to receive partnership is different from trying to catch a man. When I think about catching a man, I think of hunting down and taming a wild animal, usually through trickery and other how-to shenanigans. We're more interested in the chase and easing feelings of loneliness than we are about building a life with another person. When I think about opening to receive a partnership, though, it's about being visible. It's about showing up as the authentic *you* in the relationship. It's not about games, manipulation or filling a void, but about a willingness and readiness to receive love and happiness. When you start from this place, you will almost always attract the relationship that will feed and nurture you on every level.

In Summary

You are lovable and deserve the relationship you want. Living a deliciously selfish life is about creating balance and happiness in all areas of our lives, including our love lives. Work on letting down your guard, becoming vulnerable and opening to receive love. When you do, you won't have to go searching for love; it will seek you out.

KICK STARTERS AND THINGS TO TRY

Get involved. Build a healthy relationship with yourself. Get clear about what you want (and need) in and out of a relationship. Start by dating yourself to gain a better understanding of who you are at the core: your wounds, relationship patterns and likes and dislikes. Once you do, you'll be in a better position to communicate your needs and desires to a partner.

End it. Cut the stragglers and dead-end relationships loose. They're just holding you back. Free yourself emotionally and physically to attract the kind of relationship you want in your life.

Get out there. You can't sit on the couch night after night and expect to find The One. You have to go out, date and meet people. Don't stress about it or put too much on it. Just have fun.

Let love in. Lower your guard and allow people to see the real you—just not on the first date or after the first drink. Once you begin to build trust in the relationship, accept the love, kindness and opportunity for happiness that is being offered to you. You deserve to be loved and treated well.

CONCLUSION

Be about it.

The way will open up.

Several years ago, I purchased a random refrigerator magnet from a street vendor. It reads: *Destined to be an old woman with no regrets.* It's a picture of a woman standing with her arms stretched to the ocean. It caught my eye because the woman looked free, and the ocean seemed endless, filled with possibilities.

In my current life, I have tried my best to live life on my own terms and to follow my heart. At the age of seventeen, I left home in search of a better tomorrow—and found it. I have pursued and obtained a PhD. I have traveled the world many times solo or with my dearest friends to Paris, Amsterdam, and London; to Belize, Africa, Italy, Mexico, Spain and Belgium. I've also purchased three homes in communities where I dreamed of living. My biggest *Me First* moment came when I decided to become a single mother by choice and gave birth to my twins Charli and Parker; it was the best and toughest decision I have ever made.

What's so amazing about my life so far, I believe, is that I didn't start out with a leg up. I started out with exactly zero dollars and no clue about how to get from where I was to where I wanted to be. I just moved with the conviction of what I wanted to see, do or have in my life, and the world opened up to me. As I have attempted to lay out in *Me First*, this is the only way I know to truly have the life that I want and to be happy.

For the most part, things have gone well. Still, I'd be less than honest if I said there haven't been bumps in the road or times that I have been filled with paralyzing doubt. During these times, I take time out to re-center, remember who I am and what I want, and get back out there. I also turn to the source of all things for guidance, love and support.

I am truly a woman of my times—and so are we all. My mother did what was possible for her and many of the women of her times. My life and yours are a reflection of the roads they have traveled and the walls they have knocked down. We owe it to them to be happy, live well and to create our lives exactly as we want them. They wouldn't expect anything less from us.

ACKNOWLEDGMENTS

This book would have not been possible without the unwavering support of my family and friends. I am forever grateful to my literary agent Marie Brown, whose advice, support, and critical feedback set me on a path to realizing my true potential as a writer.

This book is especially for all of my homegirls (in order of appearance in my life): Eileen LaToya Atkins, my first and truest best friend, Erica "E-dogg" Smith, Melanie Jackson-Hicks, Yolanda Barker, Zeal Harris, Shakira Washington, Joy Zarembka, Amoretta Morris, M'Bwende Anderson, Leandre Fields, Sonya Shields, Tamara Wilds-Lawson, Robyn Epstein, Lisa Coleman, Gina Charbonnet, Shauna Brown, Torkwase Dyson, Lateefah Simon, Lisa Rast, Benita Miller, Joanne Smith, Kim Ransom, Colleen Coffey and Miyoshi Stith. You all are proof that girls can be friends and become women together. I love you all dearly.

Thanks also to my mentors, whose wisdom and guidance I absorbed like a sponge: Ms. Slaughter, Blythe Anderson, Roylestine Bowman, Clarence Lee, Joseph McCormick, Bonnie Thornton Dill, Beverly Guy Sheftall, Linda Faye Williams, Walter Stafford, Ronald Walters, Inca Mohamed, Elsa Rios, Pat White, Ana Oliviera and Linda Basch. On your shoulders I stand.

Also, specials thanks and much gratitude to Shakira Gavin, Jennifer Agmi and Terrie Williams who read early versions of the book and encouraged me to keep going.

Lastly, thanks to the two women who know me best in this world, my mother Joyce Elaine Fleming and my paternal grandmother Melvina Mason.

C. NICOLE MASON, PHD

C. Nicole Mason, PhD is a visiting professor at Spelman College and Executive Director of the Center for Research and Policy in the Public Interest. She is also an Ascend Fellow at the Aspen Institute in Washington, DC. She has written hundreds of articles on women, leadership development and economic security. Her writing and commentary have been featured in *ESSENCE Magazine*, the *Huffington Post*, CNN, MSNBC, NPR, the *Nation*, the *Miami Herald,* and the *Philadelphia Inquirer*, among other outlets.

She is also the creator of Lead the Way, an innovative leadership development program for emerging women of color Executive Directors and mid-level managers funded by American Express Philanthropies and others.

A stiletto lover, she lives a deliciously selfish life between Brooklyn, New York, Atlanta, Georgia, and Mitchelleville, Maryland with her twins Charli and Parker.

Visit the Me First website to continue the conversation: getmefirst.com

36548249R00096

Made in the USA
Lexington, KY
24 October 2014